JUV. REF

P9-DEK-483

For Reference

Not to be taken from this room

NOV 4 2005

MONROE COUNTY GEORGE DOLEZAL BRANCH LIBRARY
3251 OVERSEAS HIGHWAY
MARATHON, FLORIDA 33050

THE FACTS ON FILE
ILLUSTRATED GUIDE TO
THE HUMAN BODY

REPRODUCTIVE SYSTEM

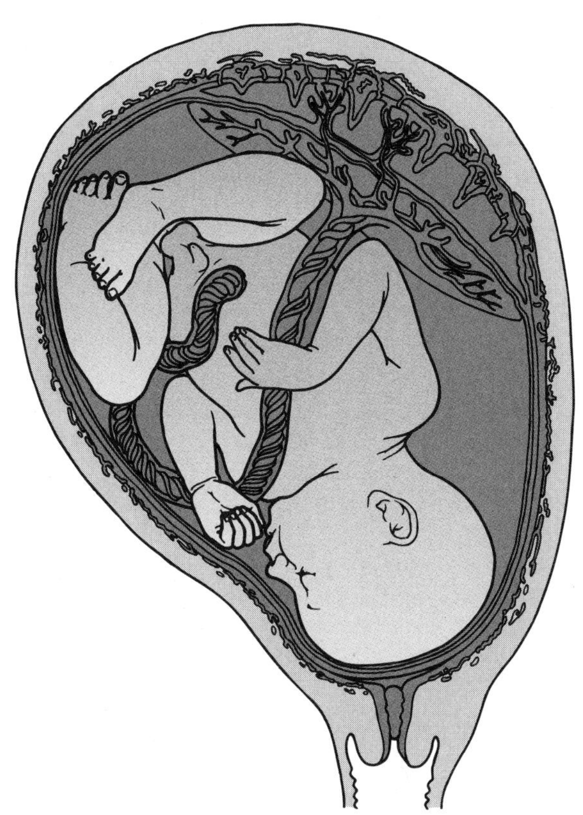

THE DIAGRAM GROUP

Facts On File, Inc.

MONROE COUNTY
PUBLIC LIBRARY

The Facts On File Illustrated Guide to the Human Body: Reproductive System

Copyright © 2005 The Diagram Group

Editorial:	Lionel Bender, David Harding, Tom Jackson Denis Kennedy, Gordon Lee, Jamie Stokes
Scientific consultant:	Stephen Rudd
Design:	Anthony Atherton, Richard Hummerstone, Lee Lawrence, Kim Richardson, Ben White
Illustration:	Pavel Kostal, Kathleen McDougall
Picture research:	Neil McKenna
Indexer:	Jane Parker

All rights reserved. No part of this book may be reproduced or utilized in any form or by any means, electronic or mechanical, including photocopying, recording, or by any information storage or retrieval systems, without permission in writing from the publisher.

For information contact:

Facts On File, Inc.
132 West 31st Street
New York NY 10001

For Library of Congress Cataloging-in-Publication Data, please contact Facts On File, Inc.

ISBN: 0-8160-5985-3

Set ISBN: 0-8160-5979-9

Facts On File books are available at special discounts when purchased in bulk quantities for businesses, associations, institutions, or sales promotions. Please call our Special Sales Department in New York at 212/967-8800 or 800/322-8755.

You can find Facts On File on the World Wide Web at http://www.factsonfile.com

Printed in the United States of America

EB Diagram 10 9 8 7 6 5 4 3 2 1

This book is printed on acid-free paper.

11/05
J
612
FAC

Note to the reader
This book is not intended to serve as a medical textbook for either physicians or patients. The information and advice it contains should not be used or relied upon without consulting the advice of a qualified physician. The publishers disclaim any responsibility for the accuracy of the information or advice that this book contains and any responsibility for any consequences that may result from any use or reliance thereon by the reader.

Contents

Introduction: About this book 4

SECTION 1
REPRODUCTION

Introduction 6
Overview of reproduction 8
Reproductive system, female 10
Reproductive system, male 12
Fertilization to birth 14
Reproductive hormones 16
Sexual development 18
Problems of puberty 20

SECTION 2
FEMALE SYSTEM

Introduction 22
Female reproductive organs 24
Production of eggs 26
Ovary and follicles 28
Fallopian tubes and uterus 30
Menstrual cycle 32
Breasts 34
Female sexual health 36
Menstrual problems 1 38
Menstrual problems 2 40
Female system disorders 42

SECTION 3
MALE SYSTEM

Introduction 44
Male reproductive organs 46
Production of sperm 48
Testes 50
Penis 52
Male sexual health 54
Male system disorders 56

SECTION 4
PREGNANCY

Introduction 58
Overview of pregnancy 60
Fertilization 62
Development of the fertilized egg 64
Early embryo 66
Late embryo 68
Early fetus 70
Mid-term fetus 72
Placenta 74
Full-term fetus 76
Multiple pregnancies 78
Changes in pregnancy 80
Prenatal care 82
Activity during pregnancy 84
Contraception 86
Sexual problems 88
Sexual infections 90

SECTION 5
BIRTH AND GROWTH

Introduction 92
Delivery 94
Birth problems 96
The newborn child 98
Child development 100

Glossary of the human body 102
Web sites to visit 108
Index 109

Introduction

This book is a concise, illustrated guide to the anatomy, physiology, well-being, and disorders of the human reproductive system. It has been written and illustrated specially for students and laypeople interested in medicine, health, fitness, and first aid. The subject is dealt with in clear steps, so that the reader can steadily acquire a good overall understanding. Explanatory texts, diagrams, illustrations, captions, and fact boxes are combined to help readers grasp important information at a glance. A glossary of scientific and jargon words defines medical terms in everyday language. A list of Web sites provides links to other relevant sources of information, and the index enables quick access to articles.

There are five sections within the book. The first section gives an overview of reproduction and the parts of the body associated with sex and reproduction in males and females. Section 2 focuses on the female reproductive system, and section 3 on the male reproductive system. Section 4 deals with fertilization and growth of the fetus inside the mother's womb. The last section looks at the newborn baby itself. Within each section, normal structure and function are followed by principles of healthcare and hygiene. These are followed by a survey of the main disorders and diseases affecting the female or male reproductive system. Information is presented as double-page topics arranged in subsections.

Human body systems

This book is one of eight titles in THE FACTS ON FILE ILLUSTRATED GUIDE TO THE HUMAN BODY series, which looks at each of the major body systems in turn. Some of the titles in the series include more than one system. The skeletal and muscular systems, and the blood and lymphatic systems, for example, work in conjunction and so are treated together. There is a separate title for human cells and genetics, which are the building blocks and underlying chemistry of all body systems.

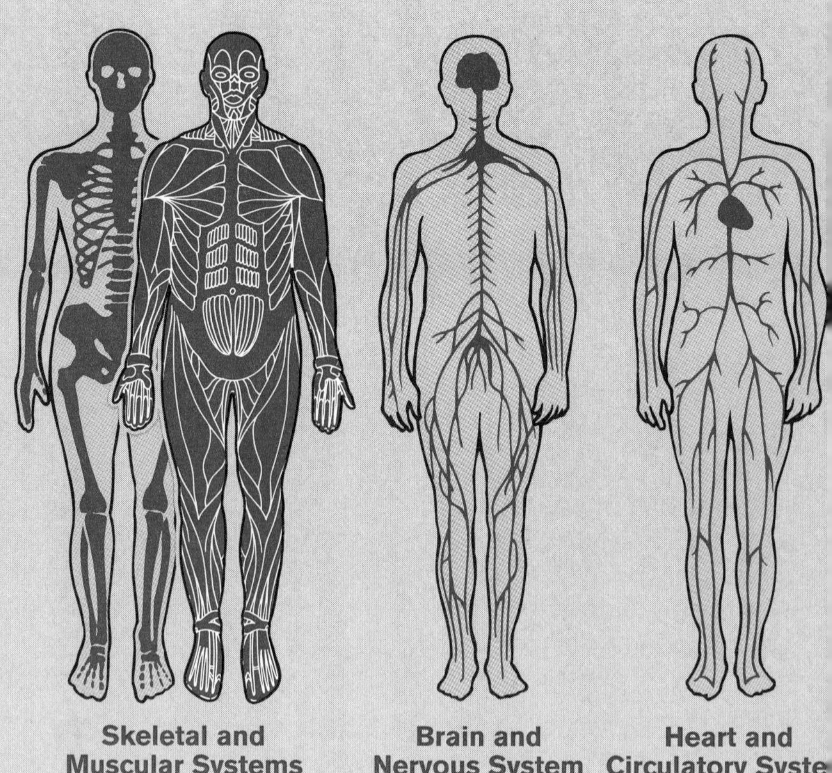

Section 1: REPRODUCTION compares the male and female reproductive system, defines related key words, and looks at the hormones concerned with sexual characteristics and reproduction.
Section 2: FEMALE SYSTEM investigates the structure and function of organs of the female reproductive system and details the mechanism, function, and effects of the menstrual cycle.
Section 3: MALE SYSTEM focuses on the structure and function of organs of the male reproductive system.
Section 4: PREGNANCY features the fusion of sperm and egg, development of the embryo and fetus, and the stages of pregnancy.
Section 5: BIRTH AND GROWTH looks at the process of birth and the gradual development of the newborn baby's physical and mental abilities during its first few years.

This book has been written by anatomy, physiology, and health experts for non-specialists. It can be used:

- as a general guide to the way the human body functions
- as a reference resource of images and text for use in schools, libraries, or in the home
- as a basis for examination preparation for students of human biology, medicine, nursing, child growth and development, family counseling and general hygiene and healthcare.

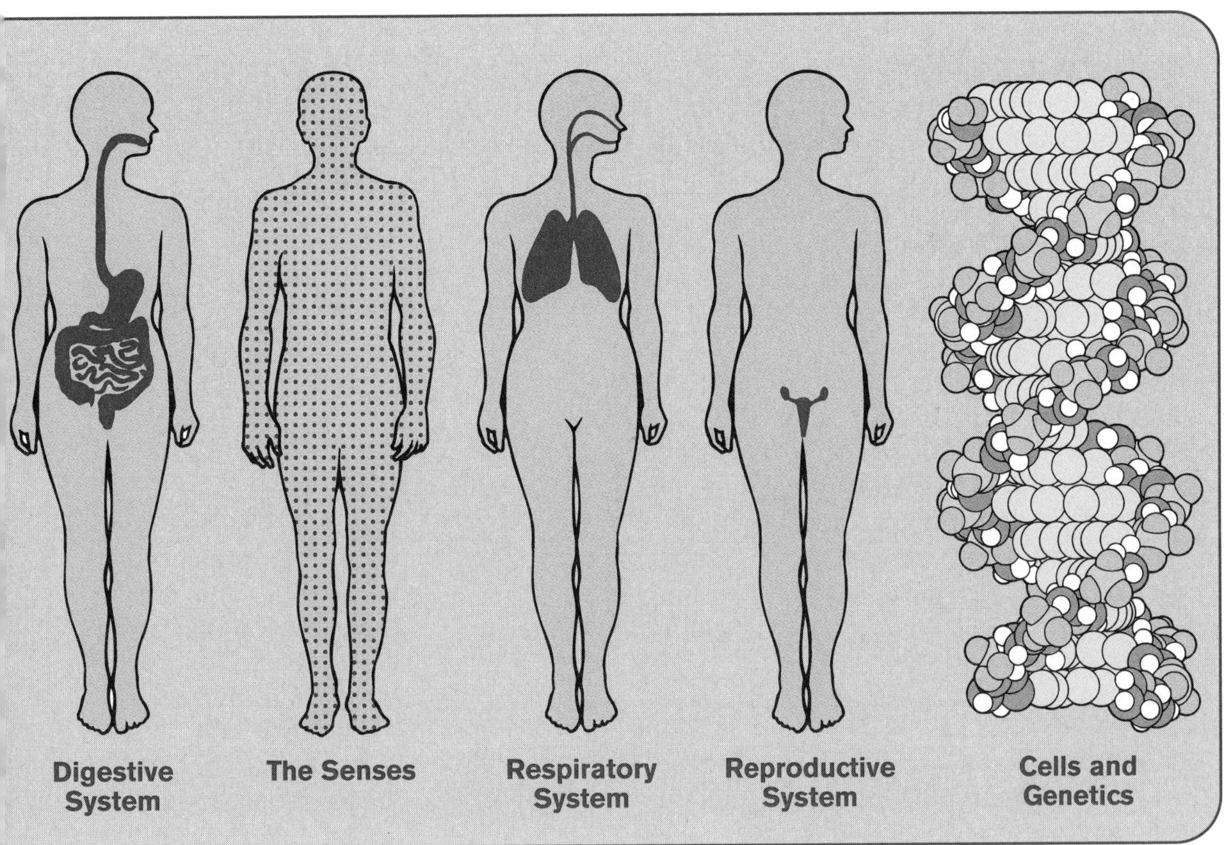

© DIAGRAM

Often considered as part of the urogenital system, the reproductive system includes: male sex organs producing and emitting sperm; female sex organs producing ova for fertilization that then develop into embryos and fetuses; and mammary glands that produce milk for nourishing newborn babies.

Male genitals

These include two sperm-producing testes suspended in a sac (the scrotum) outside the main body cavity. Spermatozoa (sperm cells) produced by a special type of cell division in tubules inside the testes mature in ducts (the epididymides) and travel through two tubes (the vas deferentia) into the pelvic cavity. There, seminal fluid from the seminal vesicles and prostate gland mixes with spermatozoa before these are ejaculated as semen through the penis via the urethra.

External female genitals

Located below and in front of the pubic arch, the external female genitals include the mons pubis (a rounded pad of fatty tissue); labia majora and labia minora (liplike skin folds around the cleft into which the urethra and vagina open); clitoris (an erectile tissue that is similar in structure to the penis); vestibule of the vagina; bulb of the vestibule; and greater vestibular glands. These collectively make up the vulva or pudendum.

Internal female genitals

These lie inside the pelvis and are connected to external genitals via the birth canal or vagina. The vagina connects to the uterus (womb) via the cervix, a muscular opening at the base of the uterus. Two fallopian tubes or oviducts connect to each side of the upper uterus, each leading to an ovary. Ova (eggs) produced in the ovaries travel through the tubes to the uterus. A fertilized ovum implanted in the wall of the uterus develops into an embryo and then a fetus nourished by a placenta. Sperm enters the uterus via the vagina, which then also serves as a birth canal.

Breasts

These comprise mammary glands, fibrous tissue, and fatty tissue. After a woman has given birth, milk is produced by the mammary glands to be sucked from her nipples.

Reproduction

Humans, like nearly all other mammals, are viviparous. This means that developing young are nurtured inside the female's body, before being born at a relatively advanced stage of development.

Male and female reproductive system

The difference between the two sexes is based on how much an individual invests in each offspring. Male individuals invest nothing but genetic material in the next generation. They produce mobile sperm cells in their testes (**a**). These are released through the penis (**b**) into the female's vagina (**c**).

The sperm then carries its genetic material into the uterus (**d**) and fuses with a female sex cell or ovum. The ovum, produced in an ovary (**e**), contains the rest of the required genetic material and the nutrients needed for a new individual to begin to develop. In humans and most other mammals, this development takes place inside the uterus.

A temporary organ, called the placenta, connects the fetus to its mother's blood supply, which provides food and oxygen. Once the child is born, the female continues to supply food to the newborn by suckling it with milk-producing mammary glands inside the breasts (**f**).

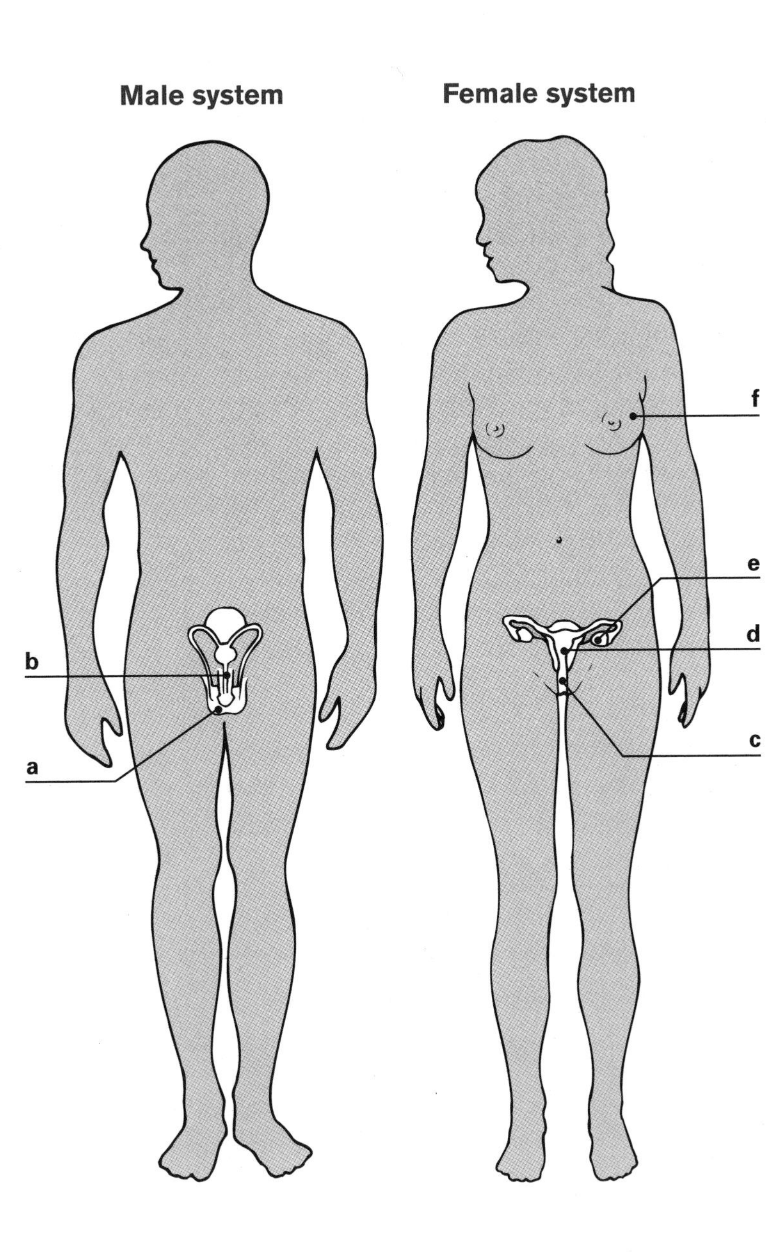

© DIAGRAM

Female reproductive system

These organs are devoted to producing female sex cells and to nurturing the developing embryo and fetus.

Primary organs

The female gonad is the ovary. Normally there are two ovaries, one on each side of the body. Ovaries produce gametes (sex cells). Female sex cells are called ova, or eggs.

Sex cells

Ova (singular: ovum) are large cells released by the ovaries during ovulation. An ovum contains many mitochondria (cellular power plants) and is coated in proteins, forming the pellucid area.

Hormones produced

The main female sex hormones are estrogens and progesterone. There are several estrogens of which estradiol is the most potent. Both types of hormone are produced by the ovaries.

Accessory organs

Ova travel from the ovaries along the fallopian tubes to the uterus. The uterus is connected to the external genitals via the vagina.

External genitalia

These comprise the vulva, which is made up of the labia, the clitoris, mons pubis, and the opening to the vagina.

Female reproduction

- Once fertilized the ovum becomes a zygote. This single cell develops into the embryo and placenta.
- Progesterone is produced by the placenta during pregnancy.

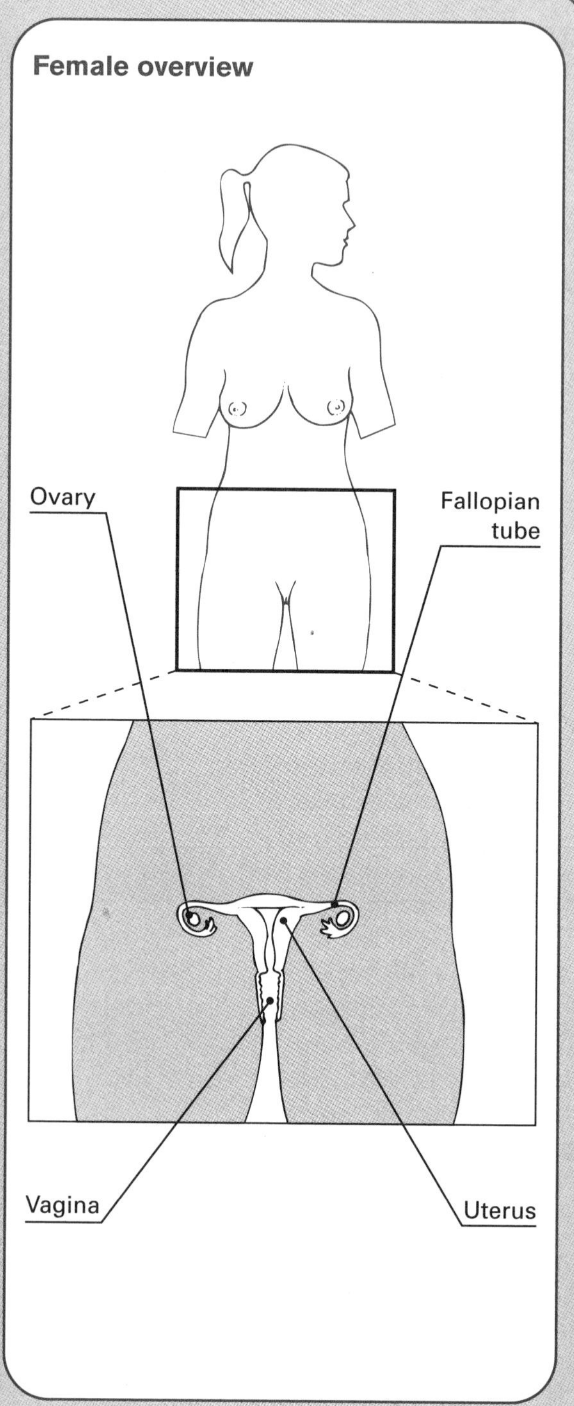

Male reproductive system

These organs produce male gametes and deliver them to the female uterus.

Primary organs

The male gonad is the testis. Normally there are two testes contained in the scrotum, which hangs outside the body.

Sex cells

Male gametes are called spermatozoa. This is often shortened to sperm. The word sperm is also used to mean the ejaculated semen that contains the cells.

Hormones produced

The main male hormone is testosterone. It is produced by the testes.

Accessory organs

The sperm cells are stored in the epididymides. They travel along the vas deferentia to the seminal vesicles where they are mixed with liquid to form semen.

External genitalia

The semen is ejaculated through the urethra and out of the penis.

Sperm and ovum

Sperm cells are one of the few independently mobile body cell types. They are propelled by a tail-like flagellum. Ova are considerably larger than sperm. During fertilization the detached head of the sperm travels to the ovum's nucleus.

Nucleus
Ovum
Flagellum
Spermatozoon

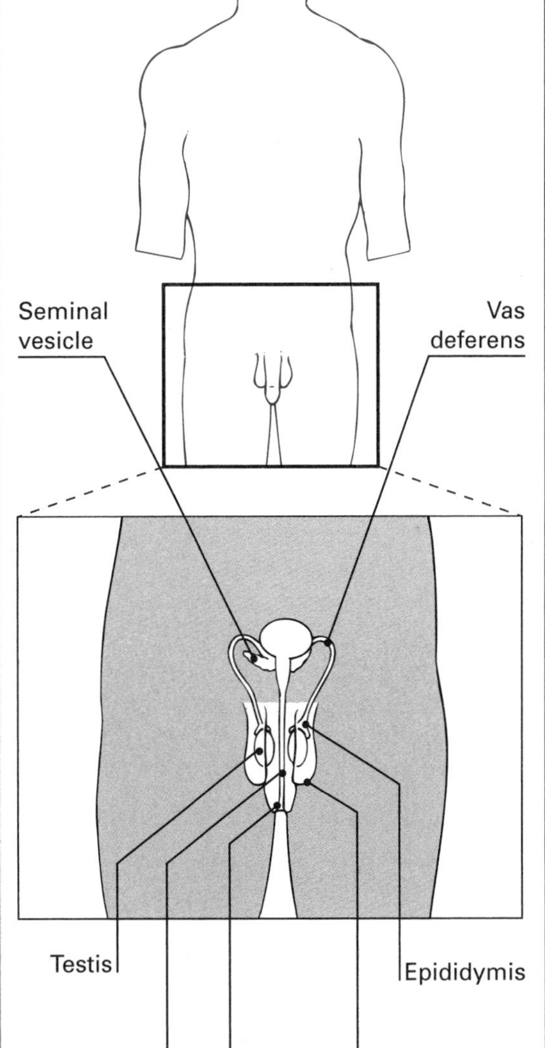

© DIAGRAM

Female reproductive system key words

Alveolus A small sac or cavity, occurring in the breasts.
Areola The pigmented ring around a nipple.
Bartholin's glands A pair of glands flanking the outlet of the vagina. They produce a lubricating fluid.
Breast A female breast consists mainly of a mammary (milk-secreting) gland embedded in fatty tissue. Each gland comprises many lobules linked by ducts leading to a nipple.
Cervix A muscular neck, especially the neck of the uterus (womb) where it opens into the vagina, or birth canal.
Clitoris An erectile, pea-sized organ above the opening of the vagina; it is highly sensitive to touch and is involved in the female sexual response.
Corpus albicans Scar tissue in the ovary formed after a corpus luteus has ceased its excretory activity.
Corpus luteum Yellow endocrine (hormone-producing) tissue formed in the ovary from a ruptured Graafian follicle.
Endometrium The mucous membrane that lines the uterus and is shed with blood during menstruation.
Estrogen A collective name for female sex hormones made in the ovaries, which produce female secondary sexual characteristics and stimulate growth of the lining of the uterus.
Fallopian tubes (*or* Uterine tubes *or* Oviducts) The tubes through which ova (eggs) travel from the ovaries to the uterus.
Follicle A small secreting cavity or sac. Ova (egg cells) develop in Graafian follicles in the female ovaries.
Follicle-stimulating hormone (**FSH**) A hormone produced in the pituitary gland under the brain. It stimulates the maturation of ovarian follicles in females (and sperm production in males).
Frenulum A fold of mucous membrane, as occurs, for example, in the labia minora.
Gametes Sex cells: in females, ova (eggs).
Genitalia Sex organs.
Gonadotrophins Gonad-stimulating hormones made by the pituitary gland.
Gonads The primary reproductive organs. In females these are the ovaries.
Graafian follicle (*or* Vesicular follicle) A tiny vesicle (small fluid-containing sac) in

Breast

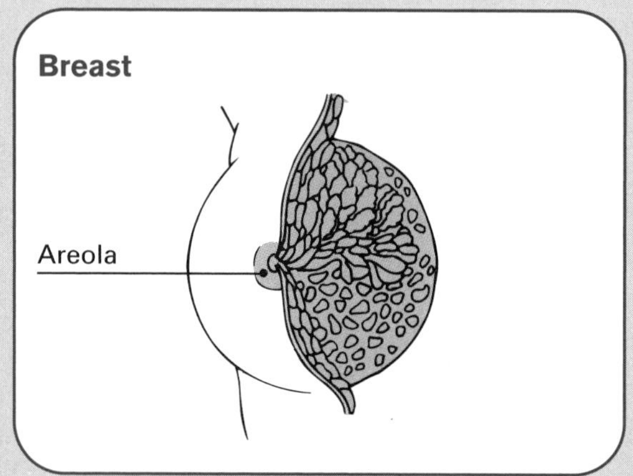

Fallopian tubes

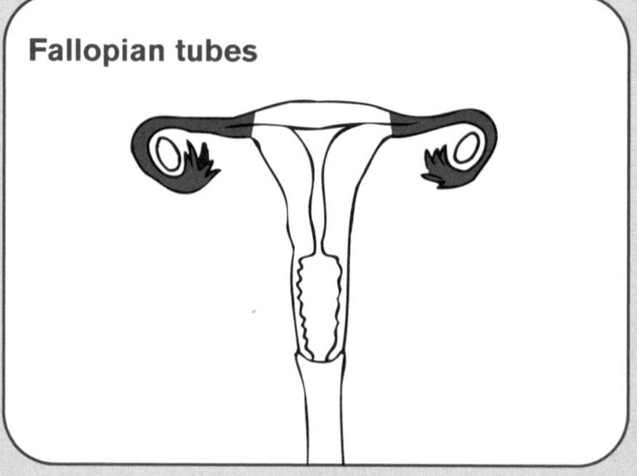

the ovary that encloses a developing ova. The follicle becomes a corpus luteum (a hormone-producing body) after ovulation.
Hymen A perforated membrane that may cover or partly cover the opening of the vagina.
Labia Meaning "lips" in Latin, the labia majora and labia minora are respectively the outer and inner liplike skin folds of the vulva surrounding the vagina.
Lactation Milk production by the mammary glands.
Lactiferous ducts The tubes that transport milk to the nipple.
Luteinizing hormone (**LH**) A pituitary hormone that in females helps to make ova mature and triggers ovulation. It acts with follicle-stimulating hormone (FSH) to regulate the ovarian cycle.
Mammary glands The milk-producing structures in the breast.
Menarche When a girl first starts to have menstrual periods.
Menopause When a woman ceases to have menstrual periods.
Menstruation Menstrual periods: the regular flow of blood and shedding of the uterine lining from the vagina of nonpregnant females between menarche and menopause.

Ovaries

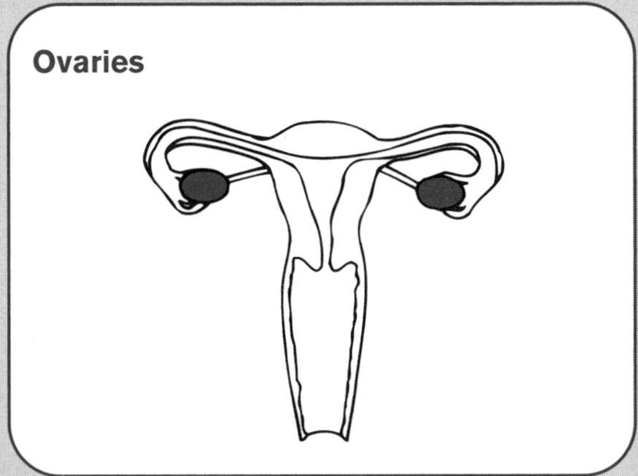

Mons pubis A fatty pad over the point where the pubic bones meet.
Nipple The conical projection on a breast, which contains the outlets of the lactiferous (milk) ducts.
Oocyte An immature ovum (egg).
Ovarian cycle The monthly cycle by which eggs develop and are released from the ovary in females between menarche and menopause.
Ovary A walnut-sized sex organ that produces ova (eggs). The ovaries are located one on each side of the uterus.
Oviducts *See* **Fallopian tubes**.
Ovulation The release of a ripe egg from a female's ovary.
Ovum An egg; a female sex cell (plural: ova).
Perineum The part of the body between the anus and the genitals.
Progesterone A female sex hormone that helps prepare the uterus to receive a fertilized egg. It is also produced by the placenta during pregnancy.
Pudendum *See* **Vulva**.
Uterine tubes *See* **Fallopian tubes**.
Uterus (*or* Womb) Commonly known as the womb. The uterus is a hollow muscular organ located above the bladder. Inside it, a fertilized ovum develops into a fetus, and eventually becomes a baby.
Vagina The muscular passage between the vulva and cervix (neck of the uterus). Babies travel down the vagina during birth.
Vesicular follicle *See* **Graafian follicle**.
Vulva (*or* Pudendum) The external female genitals, comprising the labia, clitoris, and mons pubis.
Womb *See* **Uterus**.

© DIAGRAM

Male reproductive system key words

Corpus cavernosum One of the two cylindrical channels forming part of the erectile tissue of the penis (plural: corpora cavernosa).

Corpus spongiosum A single channel surrounding the urethra that is part of the erectile tissue of the penis.

Cowper's glands A pair of small glands opening into the urethra at the base of the penis. Their secretions form a small part of seminal fluid.

Cremaster muscle A thin layer of muscle looping over the spermatic cord. It pulls up the testis when it contracts.

Dartos muscle A thin layer of muscle under the skin of the scrotum. It tightens in the cold, causing the skin to wrinkle and the testes to rise.

Ductus deferens *See* **Vas deferens.**

Ejaculation The discharging of semen from the penis at orgasm.

Ejaculatory ducts The tubes that connect the seminal vesicles and urethra.

Epididymis A coiled tubule on each testis where sperm are stored and mature (plural: epididymides).

Erectile tissue The corpora cavernosa and corpus spongiosum. They expand when filled with blood, causing the penis to become erect.

Foreskin (*or* Prepuce) Loose skin that covers the glans of the penis.

Frenulum A fold of mucous membrane, as on the prepuce.

Gametes Sex cells: in males, sperm.

Genitalia Sex organs.

Glans (*or* Glans penis) The bulbous end of the shaft of the penis.

Gonads Primary reproductive organs: the ovaries and testes.

Inguinal Relating to the groin (the external depression at the junction between a thigh and the abdomen).

Interstitial cells Cells in the testes that produce testosterone.

Penis The male organ of urination and copulation.

Perineum The part of the body between the anus and the genitals.

Prepuce *See* **Foreskin.**

Epididymis

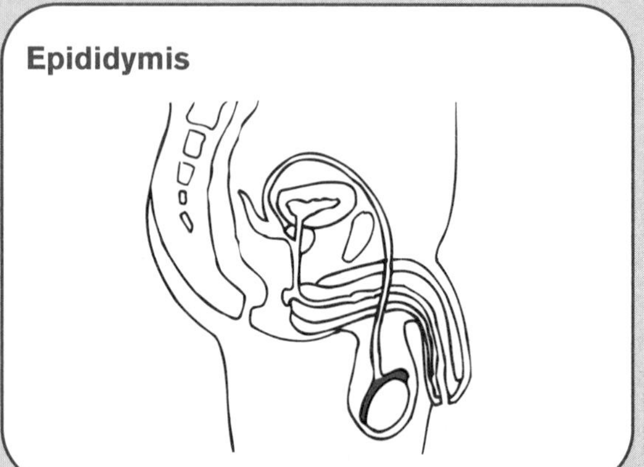

Prostate gland

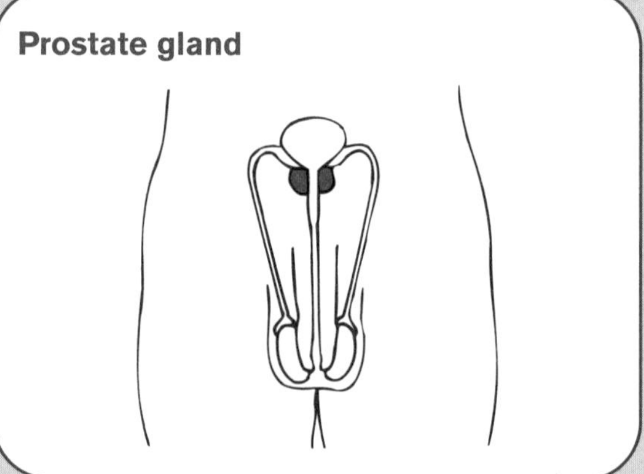

Prostate gland A gland situated below the bladder in males. It produces a sperm-activating fluid that forms nearly a third of the semen's volume.
Scrotum The sac that contains the two testes and the epididymides, hanging below the abdomen.
Semen Fluid containing sperm and seminal fluid. It is ejaculated from the penis at orgasm.
Seminal fluid The secretions from the prostate gland, seminal vesicles, and Cowper's glands that together form the largest component of semen.
Seminal vesicles Two accessory glands situated on the prostate and opening into the vas deferens, which produce most of the seminal fluid.
Seminiferous tubules The hundreds of coiled tubes in the testes where sperm is produced.
Sperm The common name (singular and plural) for male sex cells and seminal fluid.
Spermatazoon The formal name of the male sex cell (plural: spermatazoa).
Spermatic cord The cord consisting of the vas deferens, nerves, and blood vessels that runs between a testis and the abdominal cavity.
Testicle *See* **Testis**.
Testis (*or* Testicle) One of a pair of primary male sex organs that manufactures sperm (plural: testes).
Testosterone A sex hormone made mainly in the testes. It stimulates the development of male sexual characteristics.
Tunica albuginea A fibrous membrane that is part of the tissue covering the penis.
Urethra The passage that transports urine and, in males, semen outside the body.
Vas deferens (*or* Ductus deferens) One of a pair of muscular tubes that take sperm from an epididymis to a seminal vesicle (plural: vasa deferentia).
Vesicle A small sac or bladder that contains liquid, as in seminal vesicles.

Scrotum

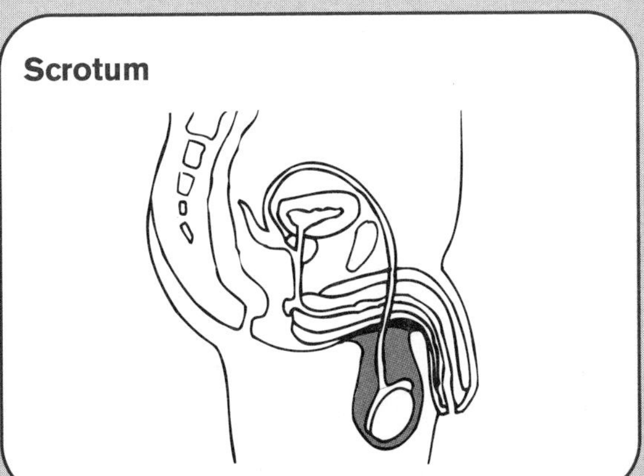

Male genitals

- The skin covering the penis is hairless.
- The erectile tissue of the penis contains several cavities that fill with blood to produce an erection.
- The foreskin is sometimes removed from the penis in a procedure called circumcision. This is thought to make it easier to keep the penis clean. Circumcised men suffer less from urinary tract infections.

© DIAGRAM

From fertilization to birth key words

Amnion (*or* Amniotic sac) The inner of the two membranes surrounding an embryo or fetus.
Amniotic cavity The fluid-filled space between the embryo and the amnion.
Amniotic fluid The fluid within the amniotic cavity.
Amniotic sac *See* **Amnion**.
Blastocyst (*or* Blastula) A hollow ball of cells formed from a morula about five days after fertilization.
Blastomere Any of the cells produced by division of a zygote before a blastocyst is formed.
Blastula *See* **Blastocyst**.
Breech presentation When a fetus is bottom down ready for birth.
Chorion The outer of the two membranes around an embryo or fetus.
Chorionic villi Multiple folds of the chorion from which the fetal part of the placenta is formed.
Conception *See* **Fertilization**.
Dilation The opening up of the cervix during the first stage of labor.
Ectoderm An embryo's outer germ layer, which develops into structures including the brain and skin.
Effacement The thinning and shortening of the cervix during the first stage of labor.
Embryo A young animal in an early phase of development. In humans the phase lasts from the third through the eighth week after fertilization.
Embryoblast An embryo's inner cell mass.
Endoderm An embryo's inner germ layer, developing into some internal organs and the linings of the digestive and respiratory systems.
Fertilization (*or* Conception) The joining of a sperm with an ovum.
Fetus An unborn mammal from when its adult features become recognizable. In humans this occurs in the ninth week of development.
Full term At the end of the normal gestation period.
Gametes Sex cells: ova and sperm.
Germ layers An early embryo's three cellular layers (ectoderm, endoderm, and mesoderm), giving rise to all body tissues.

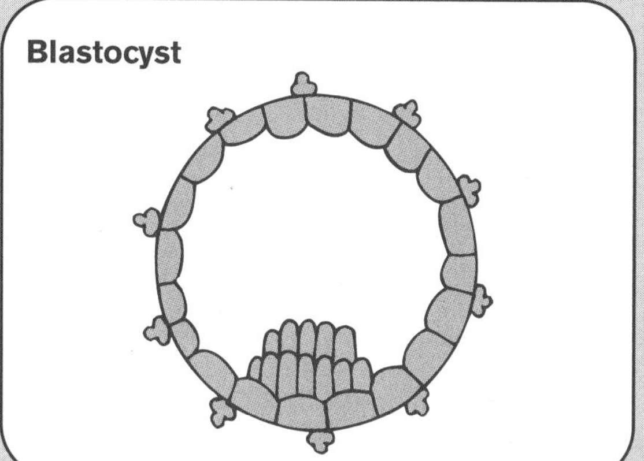

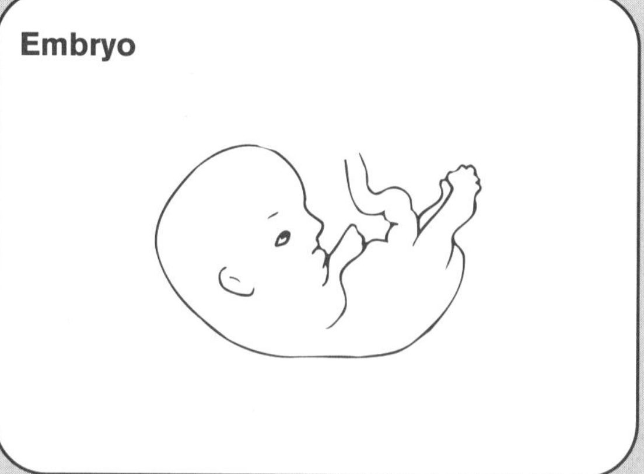

Gestation (*or* Pregnancy) The period from conception to birth, which in humans lasts about 280 days.

Implantation The process by which a blastocyst attaches itself to the lining of the uterus.

Labor The process by which a baby is born, divided into three stages.

Meiosis The process of two successive cell divisions that halve the number of chromosomes in the resulting cells, which are sex cells (ova or sperm).

Mesoderm An embryo's middle germ layer, which develops into the bones and muscles.

Mitosis Ordinary cell division resulting in the formation of two identical daughter cells, each with the same number of chromosomes as the parent cell.

Morula The ball of cells produced from a fertilized cell after three days.

Navel *See* **Umbilicus**.

Neural tube Embryonic tissue that gives rise to the brain and spinal cord.

Oocyte An immature ovum (egg).

Ovum An egg; a female sex cell (plural: ova).

Morula

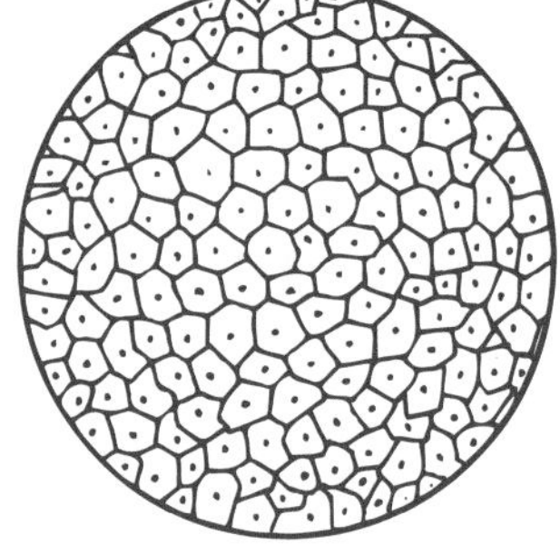

Placenta An organ formed in the uterus during pregnancy to nourish the fetus and remove its waste products.

Polar body *See* **Polar cell**.

Polar cell (*or* Polar body) One of the cells produced during the formation of an ovum from an oocyte that does not itself develop into an ovum.

Pregnancy *See* **Gestation**.

Sperm The common name (singular and plural) for male sex cells and the seminal fluid in which the cells are ejaculated.

Spermatazoon The formal name of the male sex cell (plural: spermatazoa).

Transverse presentation When a fetus is lying across the cervix.

Trophoblast The tissue that forms the wall of a blastocyst.

Umbilical cord The cord that joins a fetus to a placenta.

Umbilicus (*or* Navel) An abdominal scar left by removal of the umbilical cord after birth.

Vertex presentation When a fetus is head down ready for birth.

Villi *See* **Chorionic villi**.

Zona pellucida The membrane that surrounds an ovum.

Zygote A fertilized egg, formed by the union of a sperm cell with an ovum. All body cells grow from this initial zygote.

Gestation facts

- The placenta grows from the blastocyst, from which the embryo also grows.
- During childbirth the pelvis widens and the uterus contracts to push the baby down the short birth canal.

© DIAGRAM

Reproductive hormones

Testes

The testes (testis) are the primary male reproductive organs, or gonads, located within the scrotum.

Functions

The testes are responsible for producing sperm cells, but they also have specialized cells with an endocrine (glandular) function. These secrete male sex hormones called androgens, the principal androgen being testosterone.

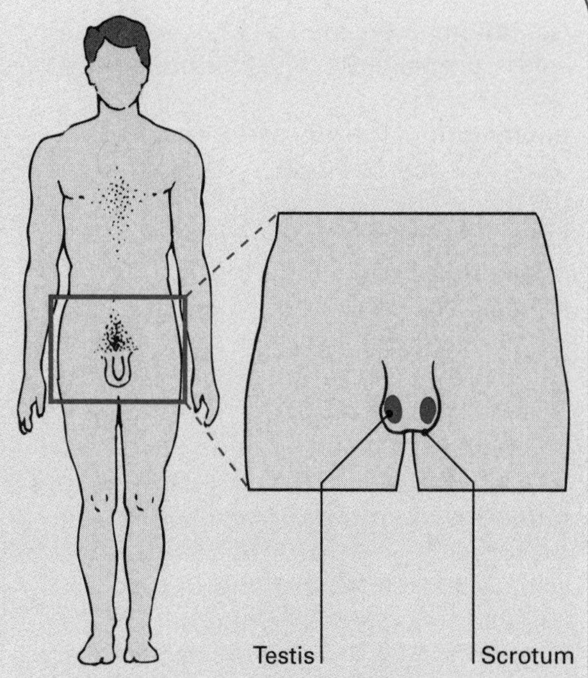

Testosterone

Testosterone is responsible for:

- the growth and development of male reproductive organs and maintenance of their adult size;
- the growth and distribution of male pattern body hair;
- the enlargement of the larynx (causing the voice to deepen);
- increased skeletal and muscular growth; and
- the male sexual drive.

Testosterone is secreted in response to hormones released by the hypothalamus and anterior pituitary. The level of testosterone is regulated by negative feedback.

Pituitary anterior lobe

The pituitary gland is attached to the underside of the hypothalamus, a part of the midbrain. The gland has three lobes: anterior, intermediary, and posterior. Only the anterior lobe has an affect on the testes, regulating testosterone production.

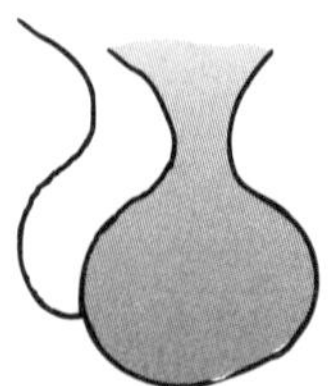

Testes

Most of the testosterone produced by males is produced by the testes. Some is also produced by the adrenal glands (in both males and females) above the kidneys. Testosterone is a growth hormone and controls the development of male features.

Ovaries

The ovaries are the primary female reproductive organs, located in the lower abdomen on either side of the uterus. They produce the ova for reproduction, and also produce hormones through the ovarian follicles and corpora lutea.

Functions

The ovarian follicles secrete estrogen, which at puberty promotes:

- maturation of the female reproductive organs, such as the uterus and vagina;
- development of breasts;
- distribution of body hair; and
- distribution of body fat.

The corpus luteum is formed from the Graafian follicle after ovulation. It secretes some estrogen, but mainly produces progesterone, which causes the lining of the uterus to thicken in preparation for pregnancy. Both estrogen and progesterone are responsible for changes that occur during the menstrual cycle.

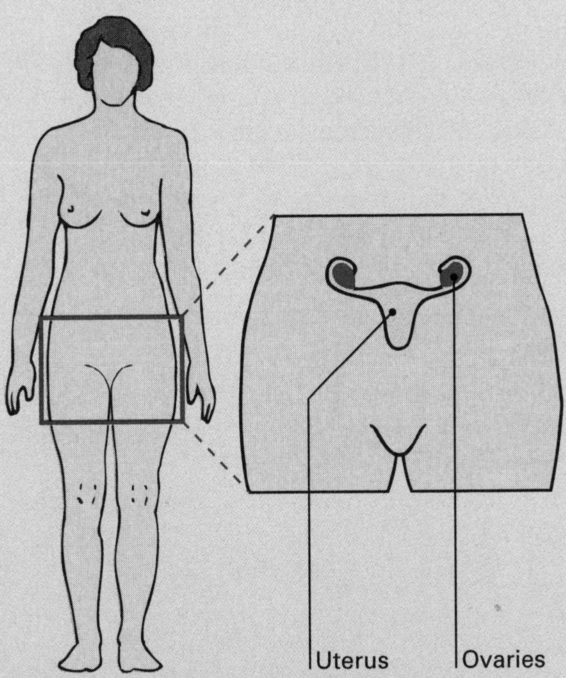

Estrogen and progesterone

Like testosterone, estrogen and progesterone are secreted in response to hormones released by the hypothalamus and anterior pituitary.

Pituitary anterior and posterior lobe

The pituitary gland plays a major role in controlling the ovaries. The anterior lobe triggers ovulation, prepares the uterus for pregnancy, stimulates the production of female hormones, and controls milk production. The posterior lobe controls labor contractions.

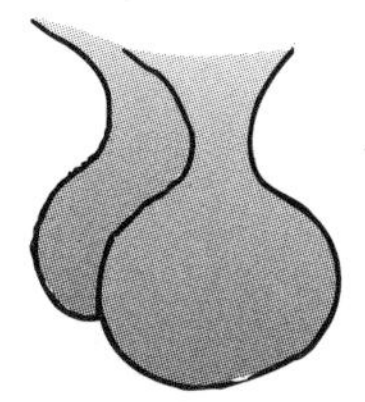

Ovaries

These organs produce estrogens and progesterone. Estrogen promotes the development of secondary sexual features and the menstrual cycle. Progesterone prepares the uterus for implantation and develops the breasts.

© DIAGRAM

Sexual development

Puberty is the time of life that marks the end of childhood and the beginning of adolescence. At this time adult hormones begin to be produced in young teenagers, causing the characteristic growth spurts, bodily changes, and altered attitudes that are part of the preparations for adulthood. Puberty usually begins at a certain body weight, so boys and girls who are tall or heavy for their age are likely to begin the changes of puberty before their smaller or slighter contemporaries. Puberty takes place over several years, and is well established by the time a boy has his first ejaculation or a girl her first menstrual period. Adolescent changes in height and body shape may continue as late as age 18 in girls, and the early 20s in males.

Changes in girls

The diagram on the right shows the sites of major physical changes in girls at puberty.

1 Body height increases, although not as markedly as in boys.
2 The voice deepens slightly.
3 The breasts enlarge.
4 The nipples stand out from the surrounding skin.
5 Fat pads form on the hips and thighs.
6 The pelvic girdle widens to prepare the girl for childbearing.
7 The ovaries begin to release eggs in a monthly cycle.
8 The vaginal walls thicken.
9 Pubic hair grows around the vulva and over the pubic bone.
10 Menstruation occurs monthly as the uterus sheds its lining.
11 The genitals increase in size.

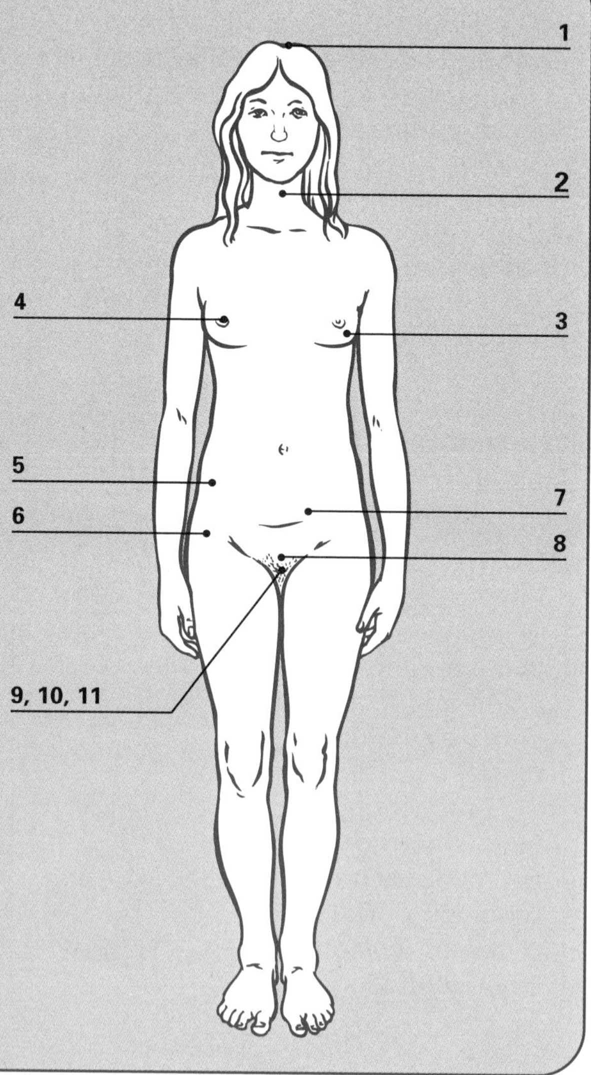

Growing up

- Adolescents become more capable of abstract thought. They can develop interests in relationships, politics, and morality.
- From puberty, children begin to engage in more adult social behavior.

Changes in both sexes

The hair and skin become greasier as a result of hormonal action. Body temperature falls slightly. Underarm hair grows. Sweat glands under the arms and in the groin produce more perspiration than before.

Blood pressure and blood volume increase. Heart rate slows. Breathing rate slows. Bones harden and change their proportions.

Transition period

Puberty and adolescence can be difficult times, because the boy or girl is caught between two phases of life. Childhood has the benefits of security; adulthood has the benefits of independence and sexual relationships. The adolescent exhibits behavior from both categories, and is also disturbed by physical changes.

Changes in boys

The diagram on the right shows the sites of major, physical changes in boys at puberty.

1 Body height increases considerably.
2 Hair begins to grow on the chin, cheeks, and upper lip.
3 The voice deepens as the larynx grows.
4 The Adam's apple enlarges.
5 Muscles over the whole body develop and become more noticeable.
6 Bodily strength increases greatly.
7 Pubic hair grows around the base of the penis.
8 The prostate gland enlarges.
9 The genitals increase in size.
10 Ejaculation often occurs during sleep.

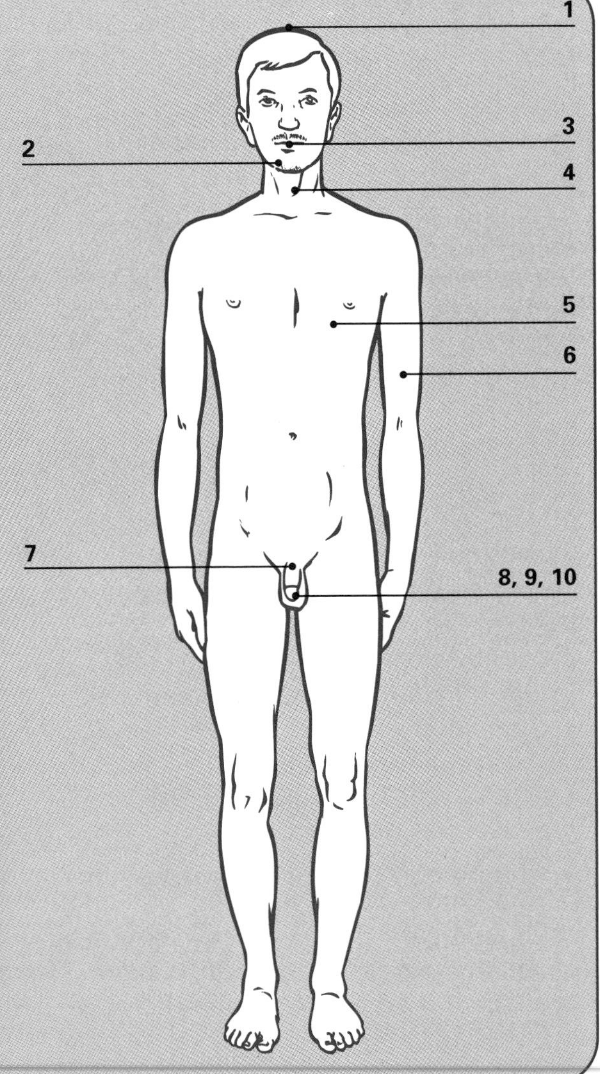

Changing behavior

- Adolescents think about why they behave the way they do.
- Self-esteem may fluctuate throughout puberty, but it generally increases with age as the teenager becomes more confident.
- During puberty children experiment with adult social behavior while they are still safely in the care of their parents.

© DIAGRAM

Problems in adolescence

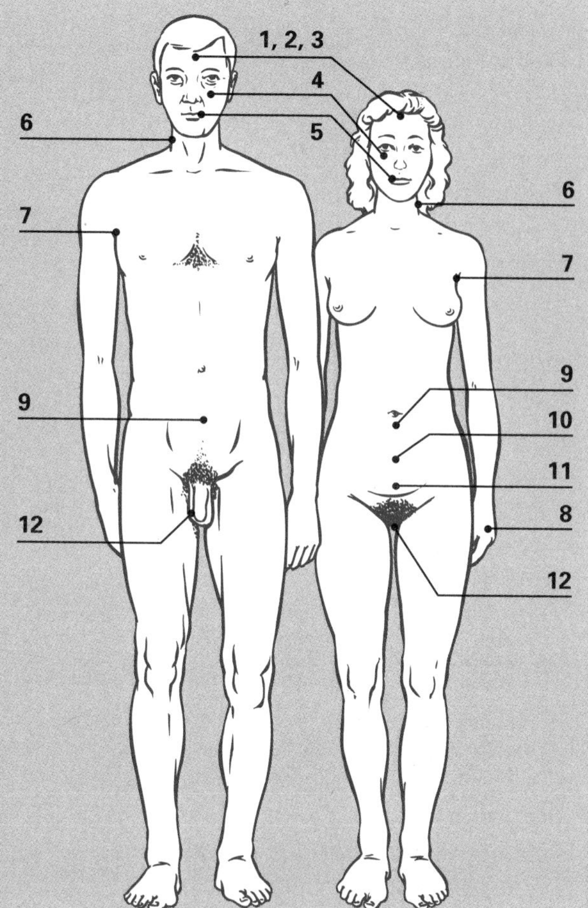

The illustration (right) shows the sites of some of the health problems that are common during adolescence.

1 Fatigue and lethargy often occur during adolescence, partly from physical causes, such as hormone activity, and partly for psychological reasons.

2 Sleep disturbance may occur, especially if the person is anxious or fearful.

3 Mood changes are caused by hormonal action, and are often confusing for the individual and those around him/her alike.

4 Acne is a frequent result of the increased greasiness of the skin; the pores become clogged and then form infected pimples.

5 The appetite may increase or decrease during adolescence, and may lead to overeating or undereating.

6 Mononucleosis (glandular fever) is common among adolescents, and its effects may last for a month or more.

7 Body odor from the armpits and groin can occur when insufficient attention is paid to personal hygiene.

8 Clumsiness is a phase often passed through by adolescents who do not yet feel at home in their taller, heavier, and more powerful bodies.

9 Weight problems in early adolescence may be a sign of rapid puberty, in which case the problem will disappear as the body's height catches up with its weight; or the increase in weight may be a result of greatly increased appetite.

10 Stretch marks occur when the increase in weight during puberty has been very rapid; they begin as red lines and eventually fade to a permanent silvery-gray.

11 Menstrual pain may begin to occur in later adolescence. The possible reasons for menstrual pain are many, and if the girl is being greatly inconvenienced by monthly pain she should be seen by a gynecologist.

12 Genital problems such as vaginal discharge or "jock itch" may develop if the adolescent does not appreciate the need for genital hygiene.

Rebelliousness

The challenging of authority is an inevitable part of the life of a healthy adolescent. By tackling the values held by parents, teachers etc., the adolescent both discovers whether those values are worthwhile, and also affirms his or her own newly acquired independence. In most cases, this rebelliousness covers fairly minor offenses such as truancy, indolence at work, rudeness, or staying out late. In these cases, parents can be reassured that the phase will eventually pass. More severe rebellion, such as criminal activity, usually requires analysis of the emotional disturbances underlying the actions.

A sense of values

As the growth toward full physical, emotional, and mental maturity progresses, adolescents are either consciously or subconsciously establishing the values, attitudes, and tastes that they will probably hold for the rest of their lives. In childhood the standards of the parents have usually been accepted unquestioningly; adolescence gives the individual the opportunity and the motive to examine prevailing standards and decide whether to uphold or replace them. Political awareness usually develops during this time, and the adolescent adopts his own moral and social code of values.

Relationships

After puberty the full sexual nature of the individual develops, and the adolescent becomes very sensitive and responsive to sexual stimuli. Hero-worship of an older person of the same sex is often based on admiration of that person's sexuality, and is later replaced in many cases by an attraction to a particular film star or other cult figure of the opposite sex. The objects of these affections are unattainable and therefore very safe. This kind of fantasy heterosexual interest usually moderates into attraction to friends of the opposite sex, and dating begins. Adolescence is often the time of the first full sexual experiences.

Conformity

Being regarded as the "odd one out" can cause an enormous amount of suffering for a teenager during a period when he or she is perhaps deeply disturbed by the relentless changes in physique and mood. The teenager, especially in the years between 12 and 16, usually satisfies his or her need for security at a time of emotional turmoil by conforming to the habits, dress, appearance, and tastes of the peer group. Later in adolescence the mature teenager will develop enough security in his or her personal views to take a stand that may be completely independent from the massed views of his or her friends.

© DIAGRAM

The female human reproductive system is set up to receive semen from the male through the vagina and then bring it together with a female sex cell for conception (fertilization) to take place. Once conception has occurred producing a zygote, the menstrual cycle is interrupted to allow the fetus to develop inside the uterus. The human fetus takes about 280 days to develop fully before leaving the confines of the uterus and being born through the vagina, the same passage through which the sperm originally arrived.

Ovaries

- At birth, a human ovary contains about 400,000 immature ova.
- About 400 fertile eggs are released during a woman's childbearing years.

External genitalia

Known collectively as the vulva, the external female genitalia are comprised of several features. The opening to the vagina is protected by two sets of fleshy lips, or labia, and a fatty pad, called the mons pubis.

The clitoris is located inside the labia majora and below the mons pubis. This organ is homologous to the male glans and extremely sensitive to touch. During intercourse the stimulated clitoris is involved in producing an orgasm. Just inside the vaginal opening, the Bartholin's (or major vestibular) glands secrete mucus into the vagina to lubricate it for intercourse.

As well as surrounding the genital opening, the vulva also contains the female urethral opening, through which urine is released from the bladder.

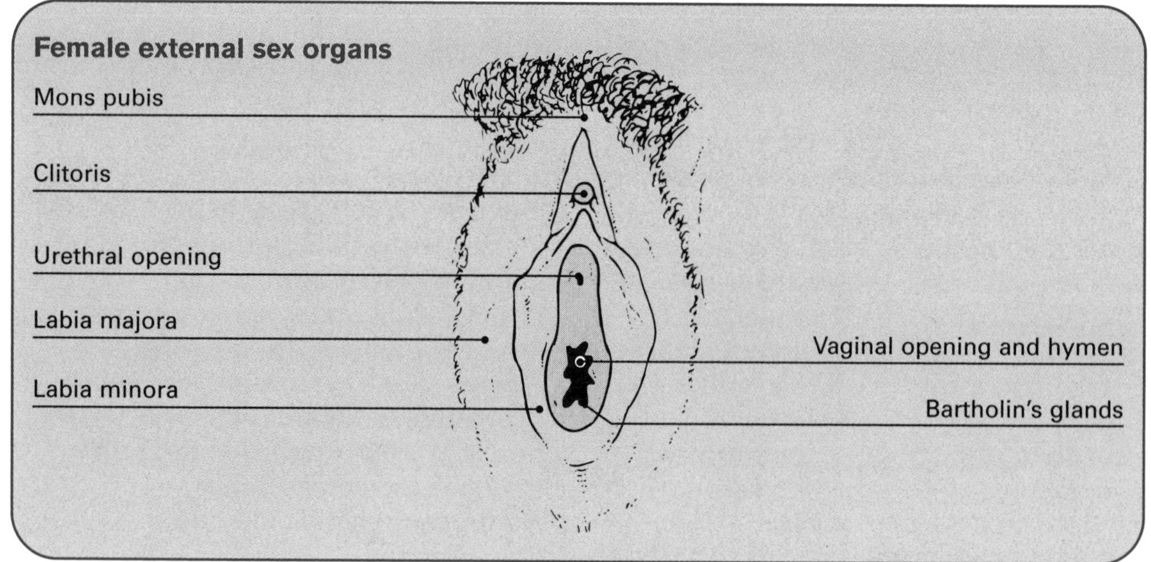

Internal genitalia

The internal female sex organs serve to link the ovaries with the external vaginal opening, through which sperm is deposited. An ovum released by an ovary is captured by the fallopian tube and travels toward the uterus. If it meets a sperm cell and is fertilized, the resulting zygote develops into a blastocyst, which becomes implanted in the lining of the uterus.

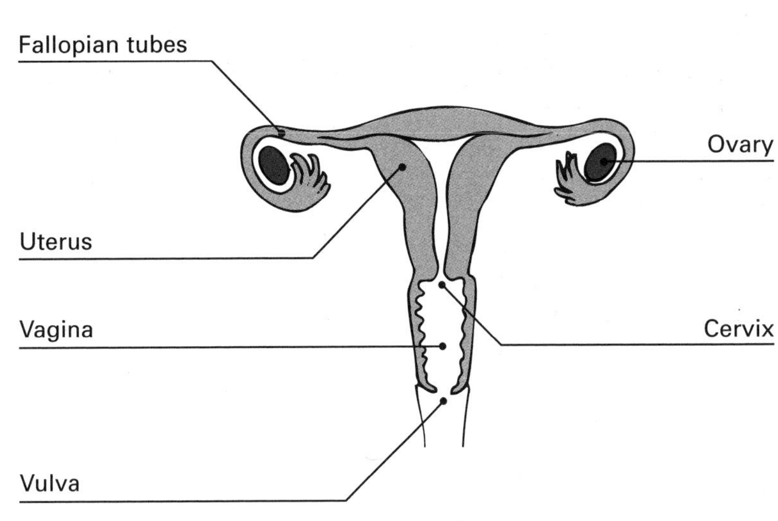

Structure	Functions
Fallopian tubes	• Serve as a passage through which eggs pass on their way from the ovaries to the uterus.
Ovaries	• Produce ova (eggs); and • Produce the female sex hormones estrogen and progesterone.
Uterus	• Nourishes a developing fetus.
Cervix	• Neck (entrance) of the uterus which widens during childbirth to allow passage of a baby.
Vagina	• Serves as passage for a baby in childbirth; • Serves as passage for menstrual flow from the uterus outside the body; and receives the penis during sexual intercourse.
Vulva	• Elements of external genitalia have different functions. For example, the labia majora (outer labia) and labia minora (inner labia) are protective folds. The clitoris is highly sensitive and is involved in female sexual response. Bartholin's glands secrete lubricating mucus into the opening of the vagina during sexual excitement.

© DIAGRAM

Female reproductive organs

Cross section of female genitals

The ovaries are located in the pelvic cavity situated halfway between the belly button and the pubic bone (pubic symphysis). The gonads flank the uterus and are surrounded by the trumpet-shaped upper end of the fallopian tube. The tubes are extensions of the uterus or womb. This is a muscular sac that links to the vagina through the cervix. The clitoris is a forked structure of erectile tissue that extends around the lower end of the vagina. Its exposed tip is covered by a hood, or prepuce, which is the homolog of the male foreskin.

The genitals are closely associated with the excretory system. The bladder sits between the pubic bone and the uterus and drains through the vulva. The vaginal opening is separated from the anus by the perineum.

Median section through the female pelvis

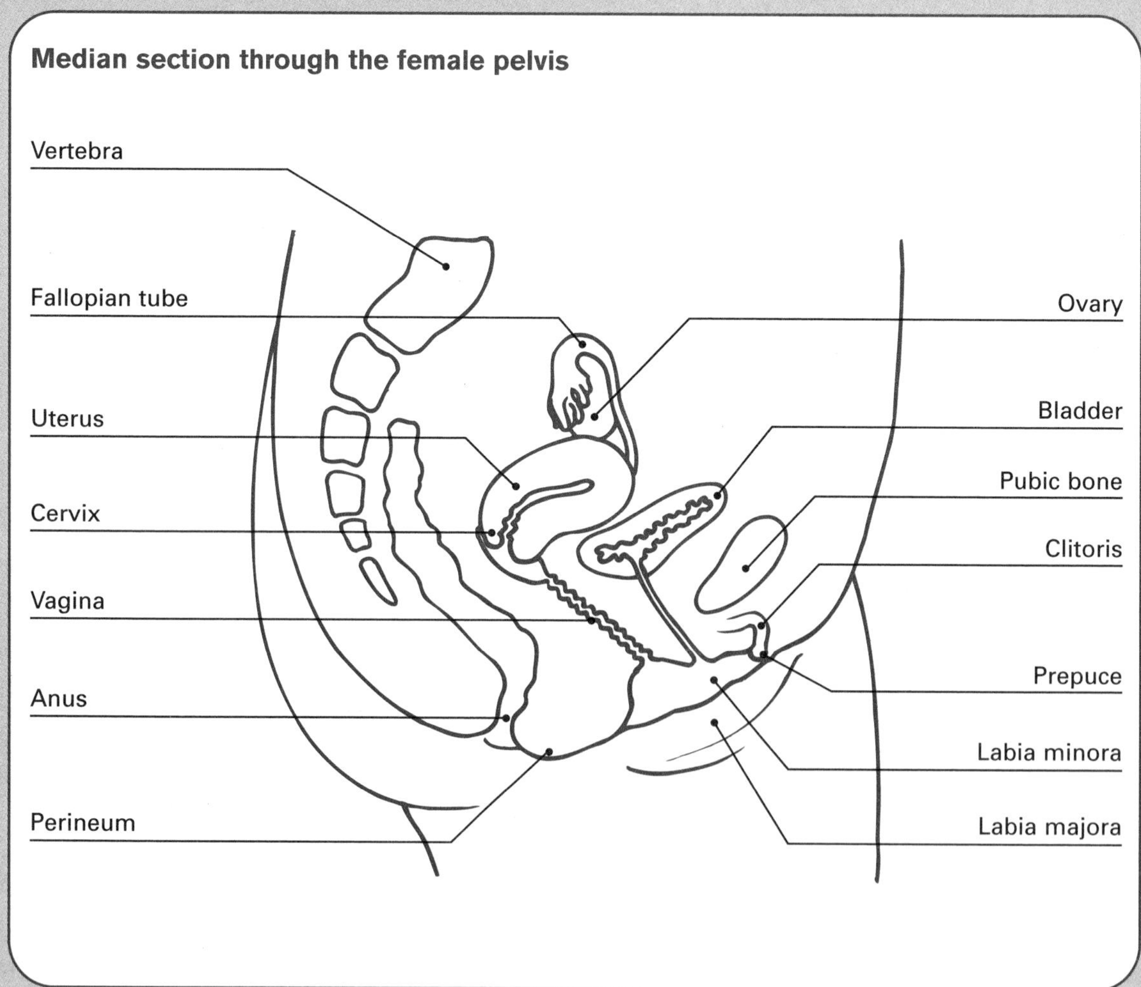

Urinogenital blood supply

Each ovary is supplied with blood through an artery that connects directly to the aorta, the body's main artery. The ovarian veins carry blood away from the ovaries, draining into the inferior vena cava (the largest vein) via the kidney. Ligaments support the ovaries, fallopian tubes, and uterus.

Front view of kidneys and female sex organs

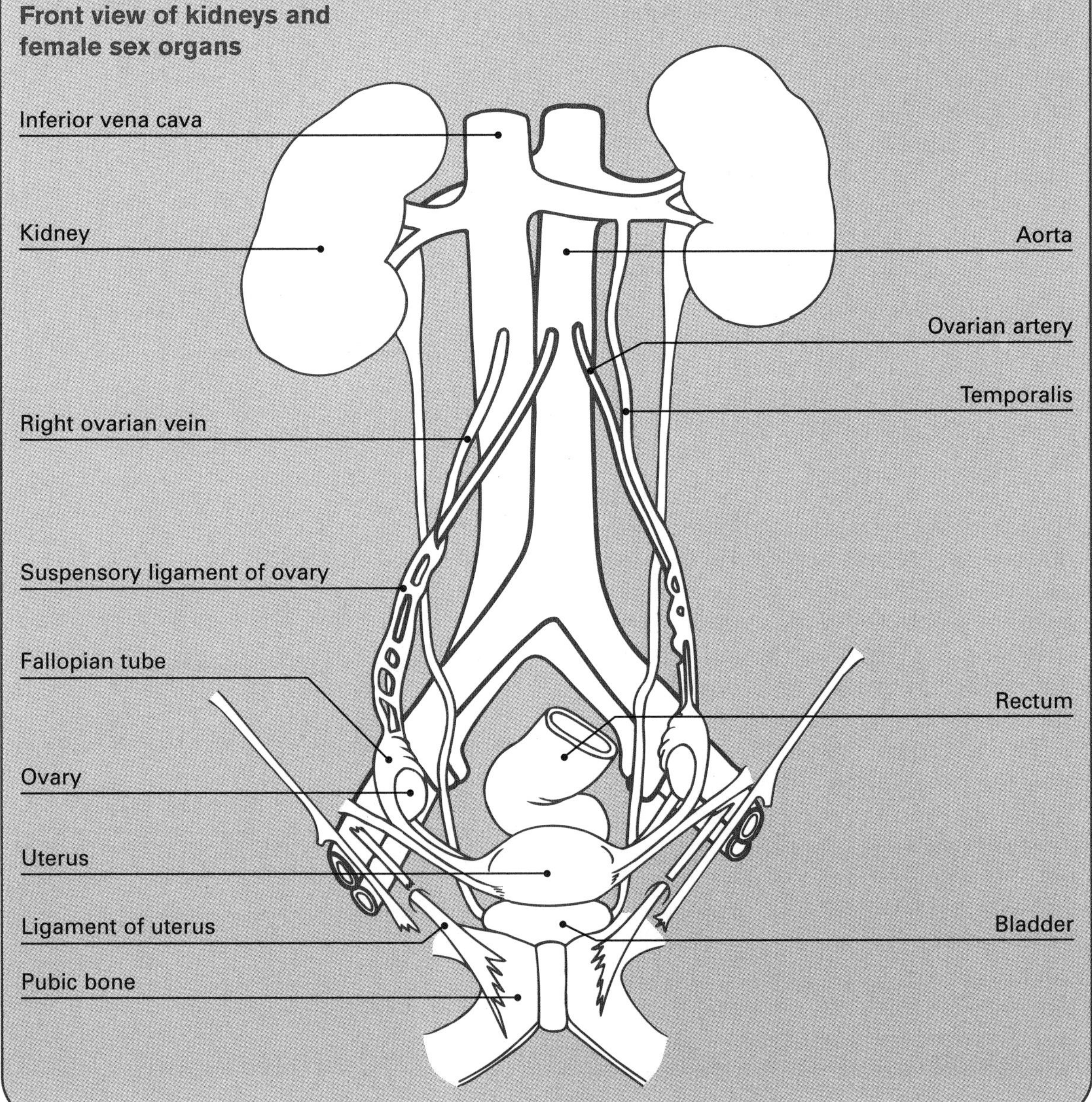

© DIAGRAM

Production of eggs

Oogenesis

Oogenesis is the formation of an ovum (female sex cell, or egg). It starts before birth and, unlike the production of sperm (male sex cells), becomes a cyclical process by puberty. Each cycle (steps 3 to 5) lasts about 28 days and is repeated throughout a woman's reproductive years.

Before birth

1 During fetal development, certain cells within the ovaries change to become what are known as oogonia.

2 Oogonia rapidly divide by mitosis (ordinary cell division) to make thousands of other cells. Each of these cells has 46 chromosomes. The cells become primary oocytes. By birth, every female has a lifetime's supply of primary oocytes in her ovaries.

At puberty

3 Each month, some primary oocytes start to grow and one dominates. The dominating oocyte begins meiosis (sex cell division) and produces one cell called a secondary oocyte and another smaller cell called the first polar body. Both cells have only 23 chromosomes each (half the normal number).

4 The secondary oocyte begins to divide as it is released from the ovary.

5 If fertilization takes place, the meiotic division completes, producing a small second polar body and another larger cell called the ovum. The ovum has been fertilized by the sperm. The first polar body may also divide to produce two smaller cells, but only one fertile cell (ovum) develops from the primary oocyte. All the polar bodies degenerate.

Stages of oogenesis

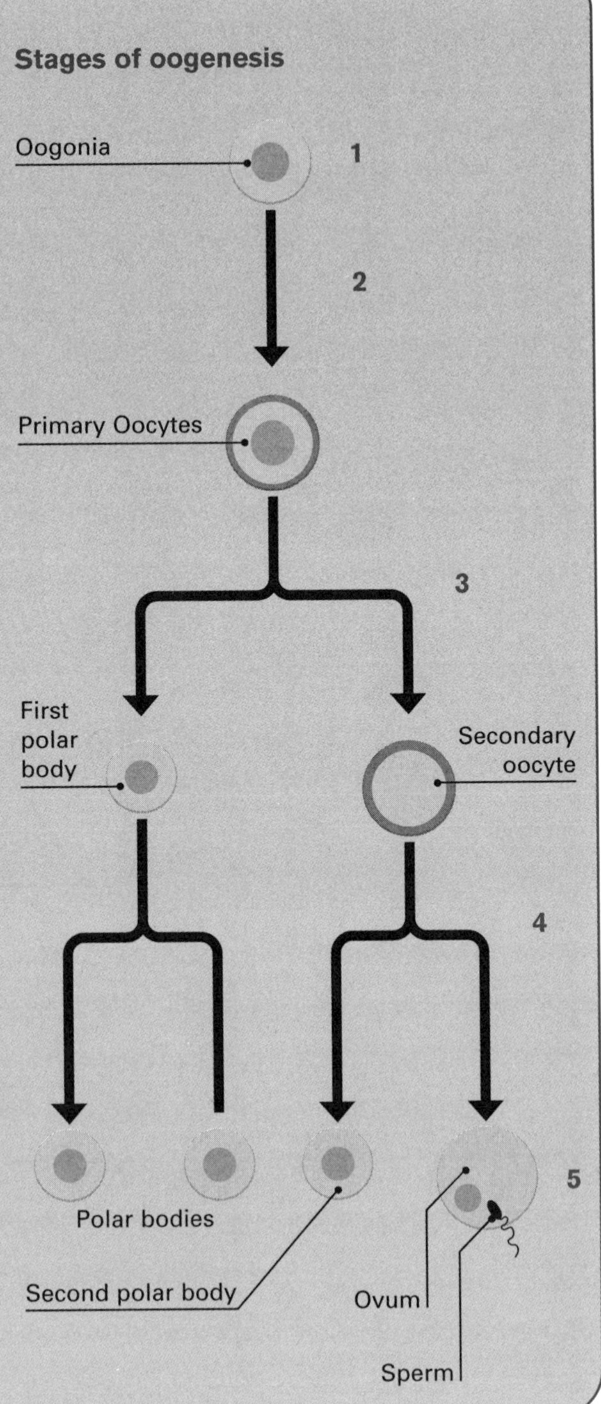

Male and female meiosis

Oogenesis is the process by which ova (female gametes) are produced by meiotic cell division. Meiosis is a special type of cell division which produces four daughter cells, each containing half a full set of chromosomes. During oogenesis three out of the final four cells die and only one develops into a mature ovum.

Sperm production also involves meiosis, but all four cells produced by the cell division become sperm, and they are all capable of producing viable offspring. This difference goes to the heart of the difference between the two sexes. The one fertile ovum produced in oogenesis is a very large cell that is well prepared for fertilization. It contains most of the nongenetic material from the other daughter cells, or polar bodies, which are all consequently very small. Sperm cells contain just genetic material and therefore are small cells.

In addition, since all female reproductive cells are laid down before birth, members of that sex must guard their reproductive opportunities against unsuitable partners. However, males do not have the same concerns, since they do not have to undergo pregnancy and nurse their young. Therefore it is in a male's interest to produce as many sperm cells—and distribute them among as many females—as possible.

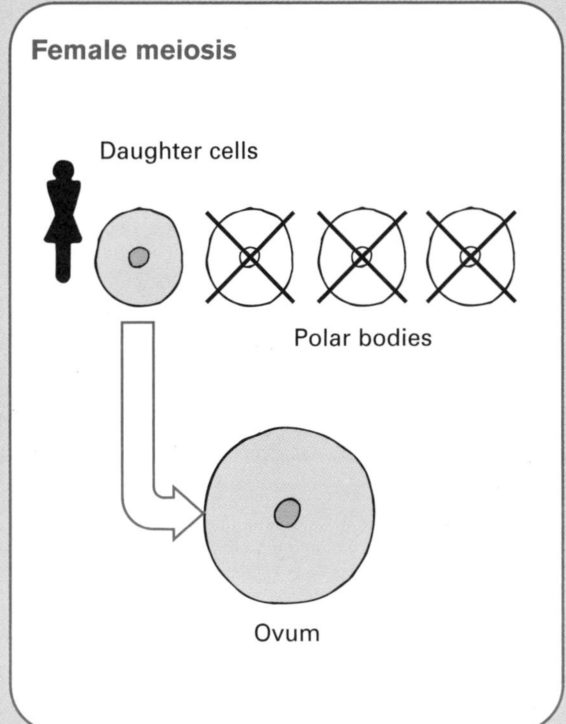

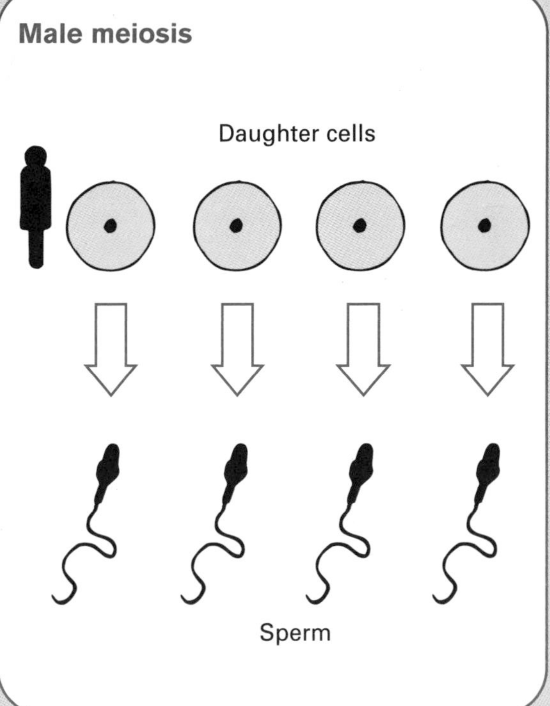

© DIAGRAM

Ovary and follicles

Ovary structure and function

The outer region of the ovary is called the stroma. The inner zone is known as the cortex. Inside the cortex of both ovaries are many saclike structures called ovarian follicles. Each follicle contains an immature egg, called an oocyte. Follicle-stimulating hormone (FSH) from the pituitary gland causes the oocytes to develop. The structure of follicles changes as they develop.

A primordial follicle has one layer of cells surrounding the oocyte, whereas a primary follicle has two or more layers. Vesicular follicles are the most mature type of follicle.

- The function of ovaries is the regular maturation and release of ova (eggs). This is achieved by the ovarian cycle.
- The ovaries also produce the hormones estrogen and progesterone.

Maturation of follicles

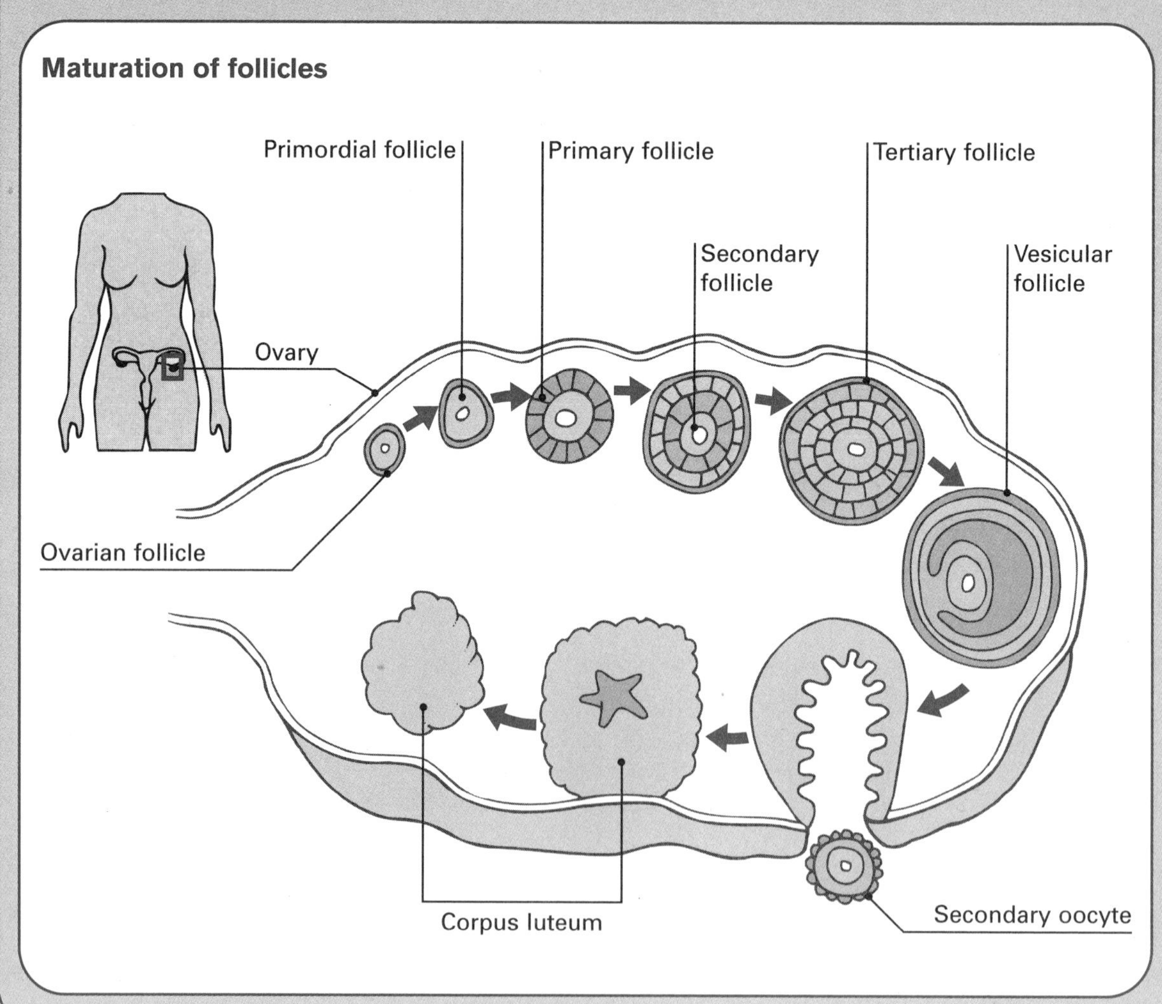

The ovarian cycle

The ovarian cycle involves two consecutive phases: the follicular phase and the luteal phase. Ovulation—the release of an egg—occurs in the middle of the cycle. A normal cycle lasts between 28 and 35 days. At any one time, the many follicles inside an ovary will be at different stages, and not all the stages will necessarily be present. The ovarian cycle is regulated by FSH (follicle-stimulating hormone) produced by the pituitary gland.

Follicular phase: days 1–14

Primordial follicles (**a**) develop into primary and then secondary (**b**) follicles. These secrete the hormone estrogen. They then develop into tertiary follicles (**c**) and finally become mature vesicular follicles (**d**).

Ovulation

The follicle ruptures and the secondary oocyte (**e**) is released.

Luteal phase: days 14–28

The corpus luteum (**f**) is formed from the ruptured follicle. This "yellow body" is an endocrine gland; it produces both the hormones progesterone and estrogen. Eventually, the corpus luteum shrinks and becomes a white scar called a corpus albicans (**g**).

Cross section of an ovary showing the development of a follicle

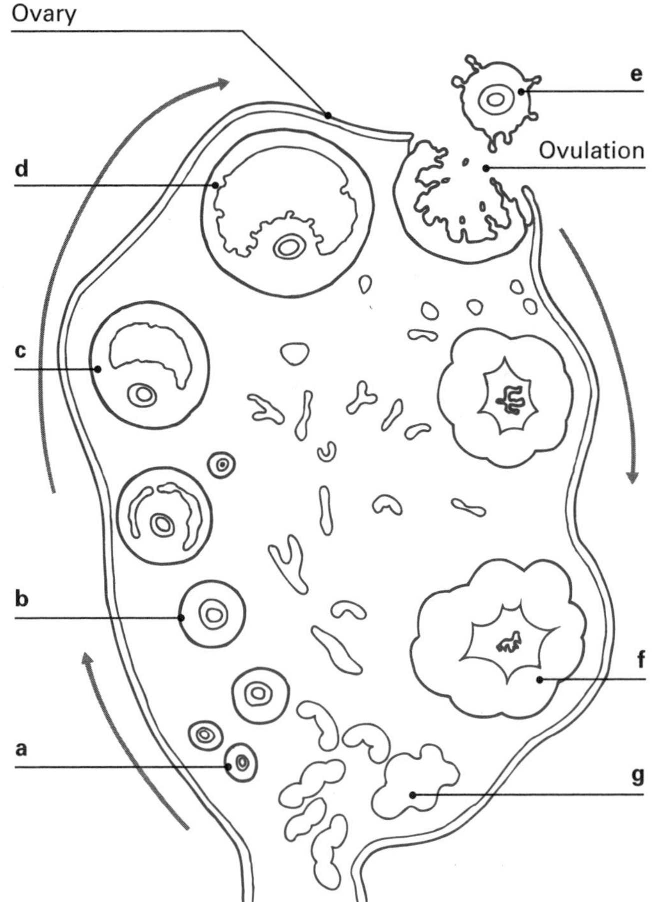

Due to hormonal imbalances, more than one follicle may begin to mature in the ovary, preventing a single follicle from dominating and being released during ovulation. Instead the follicles form ovarian cysts. Women with polycystic ovaries often have other health problems.

© DIAGRAM

Fallopian tubes and uterus

Accessory female sex organs

The ovaries are connected to several internal sexual structures that serve to receive sperm and to provide a nurturing environment for developing young. After ovulation, the released egg is captured by the trumpet-shaped upper end of the fallopian tubes. At this end the tubes are fringed with petal-like fimbriae. The egg passes though the tube into the uterus. It may meet sperm cells swimming in the opposite direction and be fertilized. The uterus is a muscular sac that is lined with a thick layer called the endometrium. This layer thickens as it prepares to receive a fertilized egg. After several days of development, the embryo becomes implanted in the mucosa to continue its development.

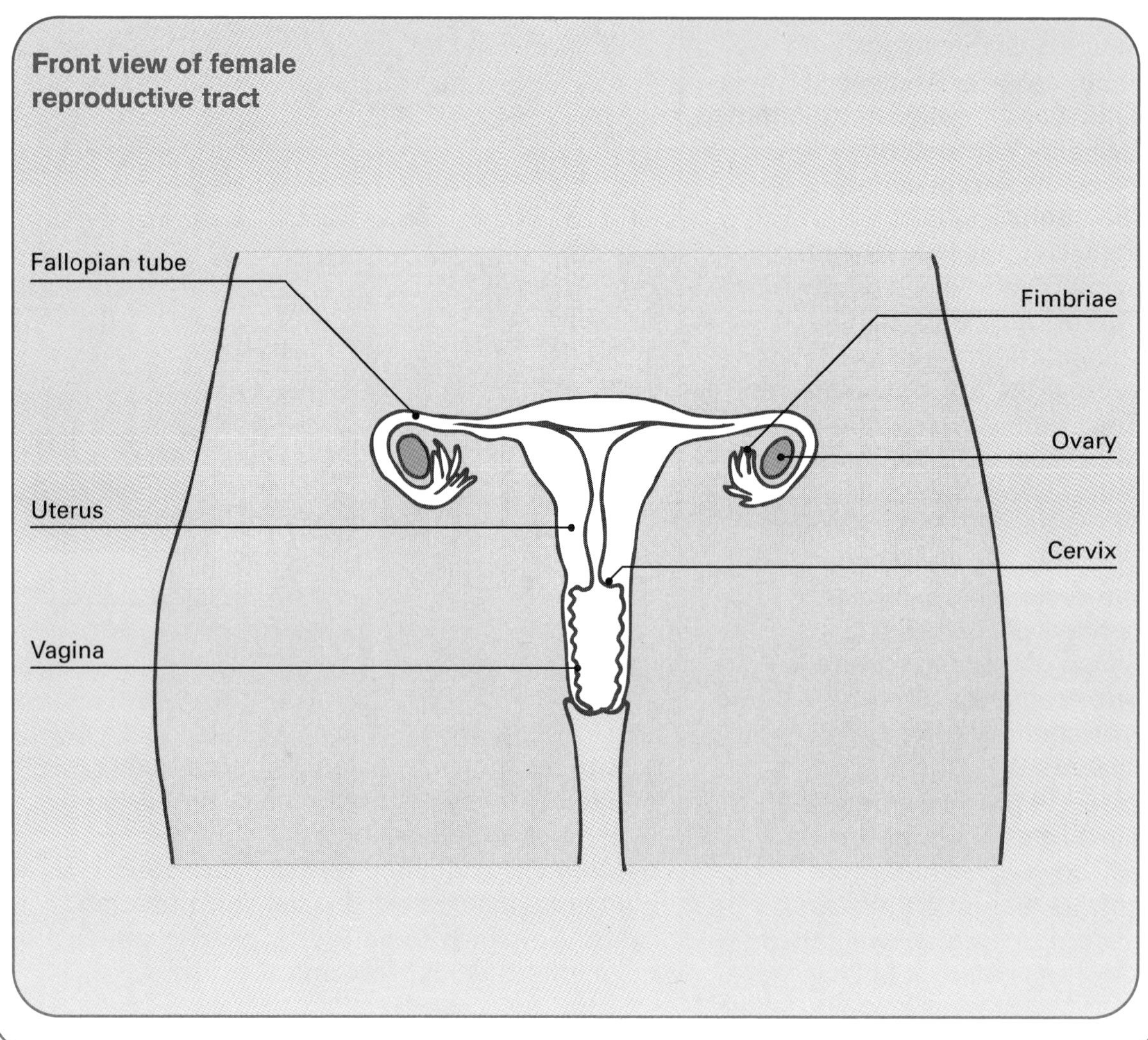

Uterus and fallopian tubes

The insides of the uterus and fallopian tubes are lined with a layer of cells called the endometrium. The lining of the fallopian tubes is heavily folded, while the endometrium in the uterus thickens during each menstrual cycle, before being shed again during menstruation. The uterus is also heavily muscled to help push a full-term baby down the birth canal during labor.

Cross section through the body of the uterus

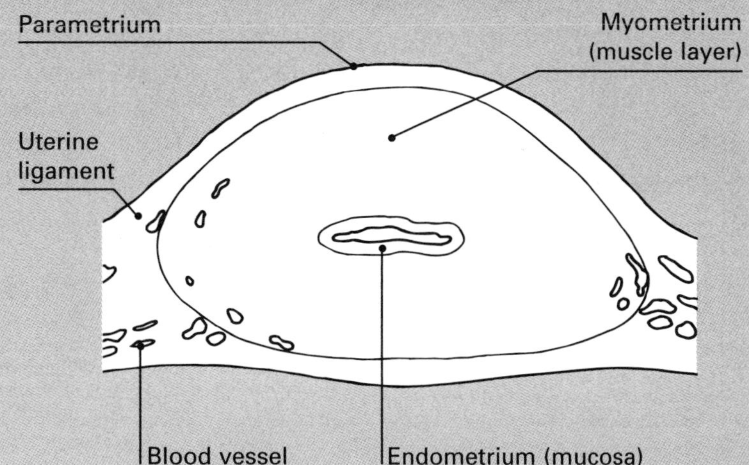

Levels of section

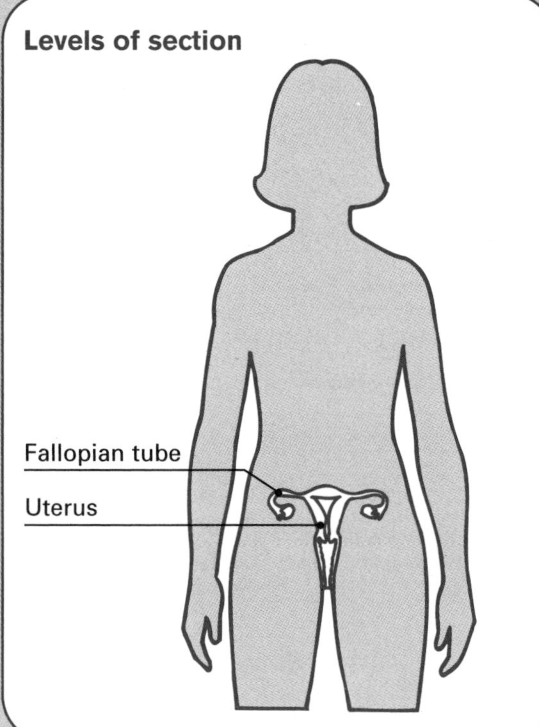

Cross section through a fallopian tube

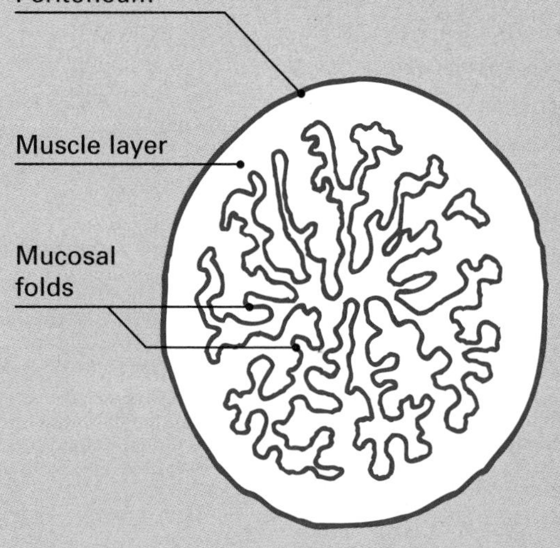

© DIAGRAM

The menstrual cycle

Each month, the uterus is receptive to the implantation of a fertilized egg for only a short period of time—about seven days after ovulation (release of an egg from an ovary). The menstrual cycle represents the changes that occur in the endometrium (uterine lining) that allow or prohibit this implantation.

The menstrual cycle is closely linked to the ovarian cycle, which controls ovulation. Both last about 28 days, although this can vary between women, and even from month to month in the same woman. There are three phases of the menstrual cycle: menstrual, proliferative, and secretory phases.

Hormones

Menstrual and ovarian cycles are regulated by hormones (regulatory chemicals). These include LH (luteinizing hormone), FSH (follicle-stimulating hormone), estrogen, and progesterone. FSH and LH are produced by the pituitary gland through stimulation by the hypothalamus in the brain. Estrogen is produced by developing follicles, while progesterone is secreted by the corpus luteum (resulting from the follicle ruptured by ovulation) after ovulation. Progesterone is also produced by the placenta after a fertilized egg has been successfully implanted.

Scheme of the menstrual cycle

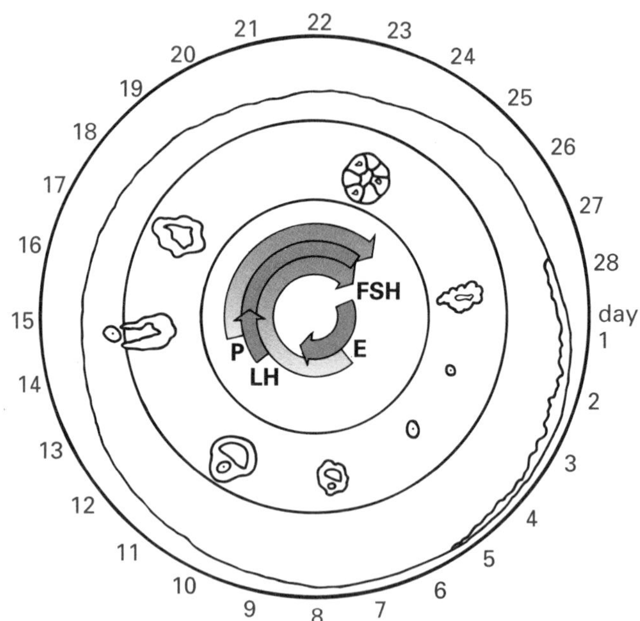

The innermost circle shows secretion of hormones by the pituitary gland and ovarian follicle. The middle circle shows the ovarian follicle ripening from day 1 to ovulation on day 14 and formation of the corpus luteum. The outer circle shows the build-up of the endometrium and then menstruation from day 28 to 5.

Phases of the menstrual cycle

a **Menstrual phase**: days 1–5
The uterus sheds most of the endometrium. The detached tissue and blood pass out through the vagina over about three to five days.

b **Proliferative phase**: days 6–14
The endometrium begins to rebuild itself, gradually thickening under the influence of estrogen during this period.

c **Secretory phase**: days 15–28
The endometrium prepares for the implantation of a fertilized egg. Nutrients are secreted by the lining to sustain any implanted egg.

The menstrual cycle

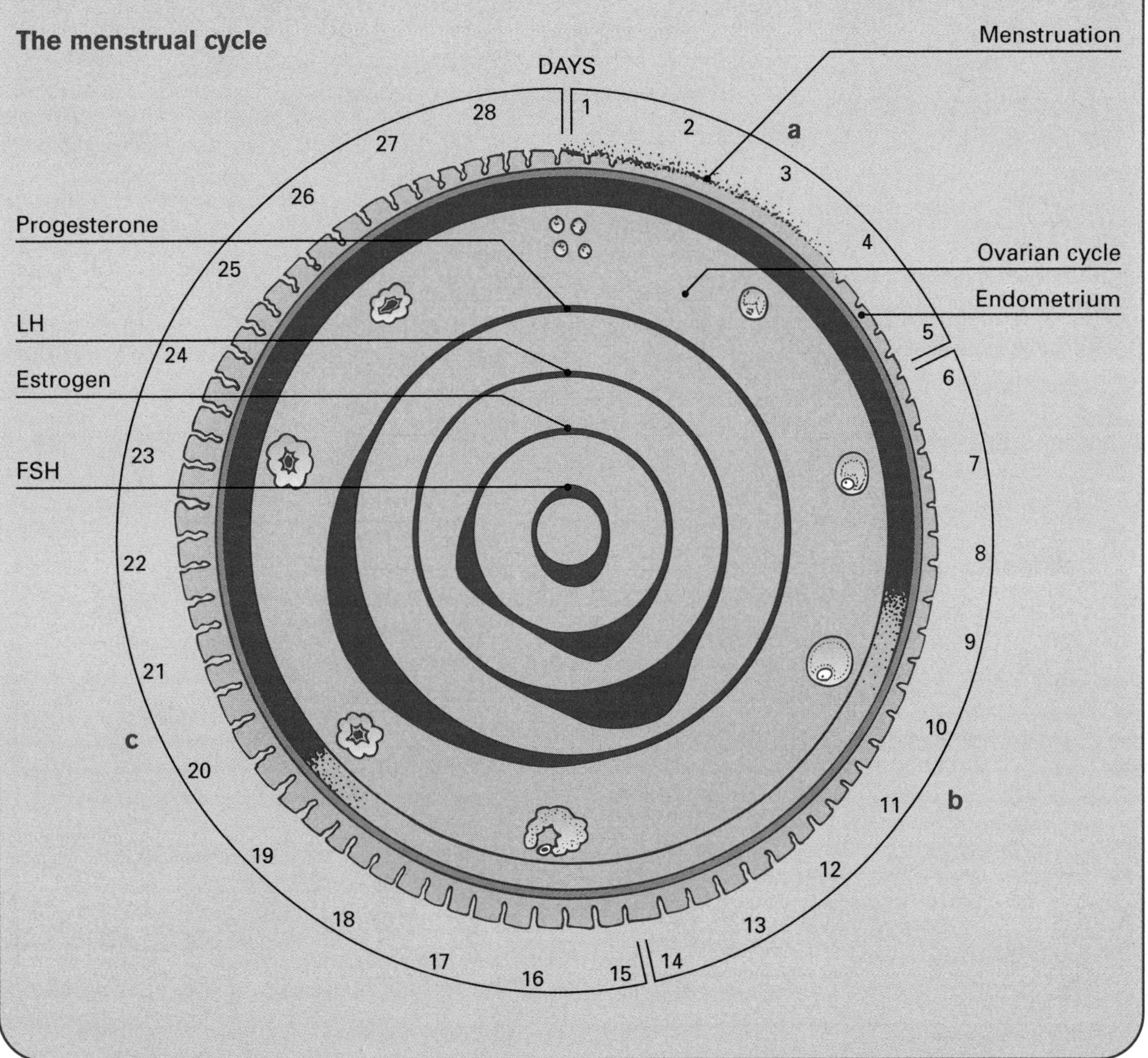

© DIAGRAM

Breasts

The mature female breast is a milk-producing organ formed of many lobes, each with a tree-like system of milk ducts. Clustered nodules feed into small ducts that lead into a main milk duct opening into the nipple. Each lobe is embedded in fat and separated from neighboring lobes by fibrous tissue. On these pages we look at some common breast problems. Sometimes one breast develops before the other, giving grounds for needless worry. Variations in fat content (which gives a breast its bulk) can cause cosmetic problems. Breast infections, cysts, and tumors can threaten health and so always deserve attention.

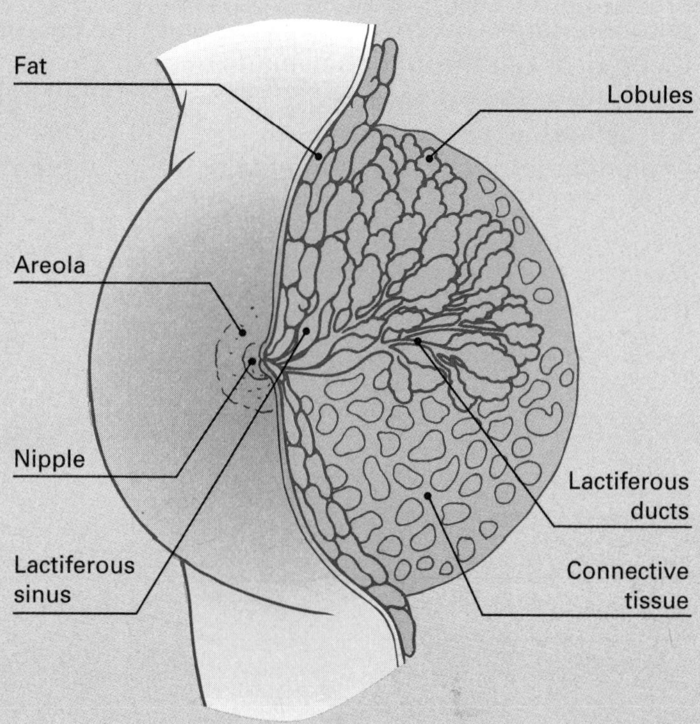

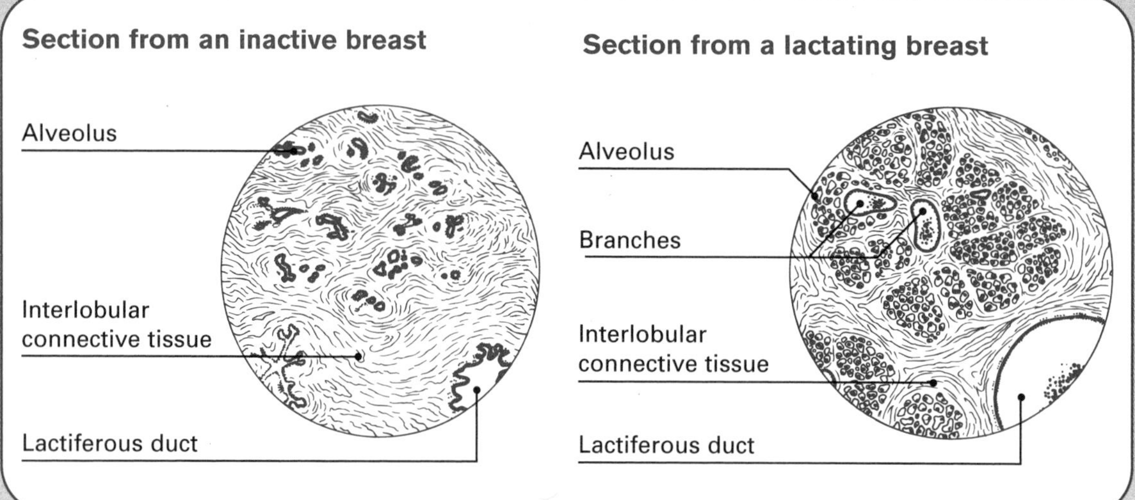

Changes in breasts

Breasts remain undeveloped before puberty. About the age of 11 (**a**), breasts start to grow: grape-sized nodules beneath the nipples make the surrounding pigmented areas (the areolae) bulge outward. Often one breast starts to grow before the other. By the age of 16, growth of milk ducts and fat makes breasts prominent and firm. In pregnancy (**b**) the milk ducts grow until the breasts are one third larger than usual. After childbirth, breasts may remain larger than they were. About the time of the menopause (**c**) the breasts shrink and may begin to droop, although some women's breasts gain increased fat deposits.

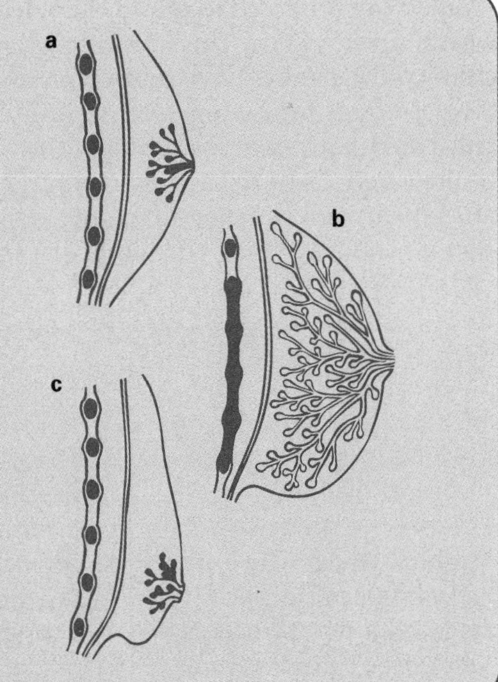

Breast cancer

Cancers may show themselves in a change in nipple size, shape, or color; bloodstained nipple discharge; a painless lump in the breast with dimpled skin above; or a hard lump in the armpit. Detecting the cancer within a month of its onset may help to boost survival chances enormously, so monthly self-examination is advisable. Some women tend to be more at risk than others. They include those with a relative who has had the disease; those with benign breast tumors; those who have had no children, one child, or a first child when they were over 35; and women experiencing menopause in their 50s.

Cysts and benign tumors

Most lumps in the breast are harmless cysts or tumors. Cysts are small sacs comprising blocked milk ducts filled with fluid made by breast cells. All women's breasts contain scores of cysts too tiny to be noticed. Doctors can sometimes collapse a large cyst by inserting a hollow needle and drawing off the fluid. Benign tumors are growths that develop in a slow, orderly way (unlike malignant tumors). But if a benign lump in the breast keeps growing it may press hard enough on nearby nerves and other tissues to cause pain (a painful lump in the breast is usually benign). A surgeon will then remove the lump.

© DIAGRAM

Female sexual health

Women can do much to prevent problems with simple hygiene. This includes: wearing clean cotton panties daily (not nylon ones, as these promote fungal infections); washing the vulva daily with mild soap; wiping the genitals from front to back after a bowel movement; remembering to remove tampons after a period; avoiding chemicals that irritate the vagina; and ensuring that a sexual partner is clean and disease-free. Ideally a woman should learn to use a speculum, an instrument that enables her to see her internal genitals clearly; she will then be able to notice any unexplained change. Abdominal pain or swelling, or pain during or after intercourse, should always be investigated medically.

Washing

Skin in and around the genital area produces natural oils and discharge that protect against most infections. Chemicals and perfume in soaps and tampons can break down this protection. Wash the area gently, in the morning and evening, with mild soaps and warm, not hot, water. Washing in a bidet, shower, or bath is preferable to using a flannel or medical wipe.

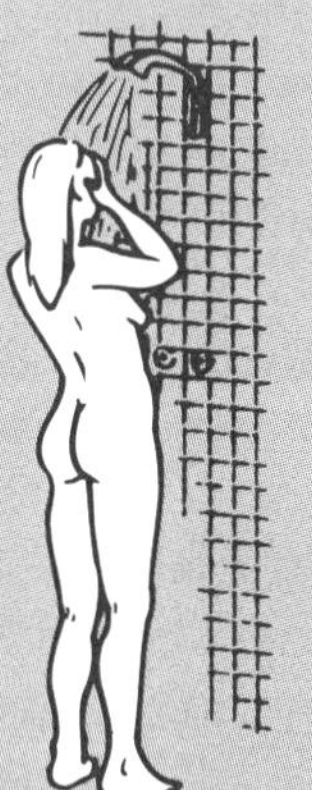

Sanitary pads

These are thin absorbent pads that are used to soak up blood discharged during a period to prevent it reaching and staining clothing. They are placed inside panties in front of the genital area. Sanitary pads are made of a disposable, soft, cotton-like material, often with a waterproof outer layer to prevent leaks and one or more adhesive strips to hold them in place. They come in different sizes and thicknesses. The pads should be used and removed every few hours, but it is safe to use one to last through the night. Used sanitary pads should be placed in a bag and disposed of in a garbage bin. They should not be discarded down the toilet.

Tampons

Tampons are used like sanitary towels but are rolled-up absorbent pads that are inserted gently into the vagina. They can be inserted by hand or with the help of an applicator. They are available in different sizes and absorbencies to suit the heaviness of bleeding. They have threads attached that are used to pull them out. Tampons, too, should be used and removed every few hours. Women should wash their hands before and after using them. It is sensible to remove a tampon before taking a shower or bath and insert a fresh one afterward. If tampons or sanitary towels are not changed regularly, there is more chance of vaginal infection.

Irritation and infection

Irritation of the genital tract may be due to infection, or have chemical or mechanical causes. If the irritation persists for more than a day or two, consult a doctor. Illness, injury, overdouching, or sexual intercourse with an infected partner may cause trouble externally or internally. Infection of the vulva (**a**) and vagina (**b**) can cause irritation and discharge. Cuts or abrasions (**c**) may give rise to infection of the cervix, the neck of the womb (**d**), or the Fallopian tubes (**e**). If you suspect you may have an infection of the genital tract consult your doctor.

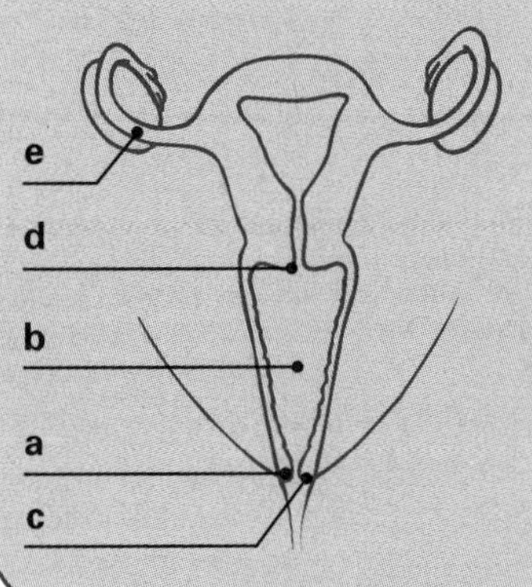

Displaced uterus

Some women suffer retroversion or prolapse of the uterus. In retroversion (**f**) the uterus is always tilted backward, causing urine retention in pregnancy, sometimes with cystitis or even a miscarriage. Doctors treat it by manually repositioning the uterus, though surgery is sometimes needed. In prolapse (**g**), weakened muscles let the uterus sag down into or even beyond the vagina, causing discomfort, discharge, backache, and urination problems. Surgery is generally required.

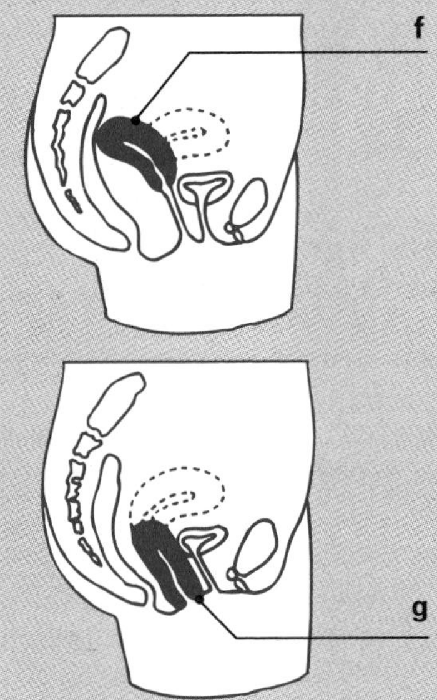

Hysterectomy

This is an operation to remove the uterus. It may be subtotal, involving just the uterus (**h**); total, involving uterus and cervix (**i**); or radical, involving uterus, cervix, part of the vagina, local lymphatic ducts, ovaries and Fallopian tubes (**j**). Conditions that may require hysterectomy include fibroids, endometriosis, menstrual problems, and cancer. If the ovaries have to be removed, hormone treatment prevents menopause and most women continue to have a normal sex life.

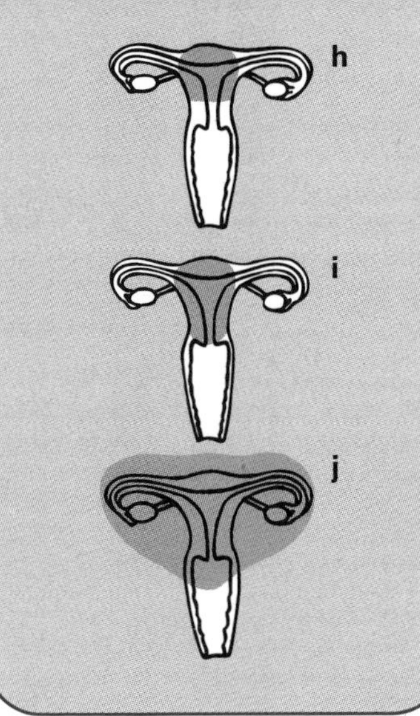

© DIAGRAM

Menstrual problems 1

Women between the ages of approximately 12 and 47 experience a flow of blood and mucus from the vagina about once every 28 days. This regular flow indicates that several things have happened. First, hormones have helped thicken the womb lining to receive a fertilized egg. Next, an ovary has released an egg. If this has remained unfertilized, hormone action has helped to break up the lining of the womb, which has leaked out with some blood—the process called menstruation. Women wear pads or insert tampons in the vagina to absorb the menstrual flow. But many have to cope with other problems, ranging from premenstrual tension to period pains and abnormal periods. Here we look at problems commonly associated with menstruation.

Onset of puberty

This can start as early as nine years old or as late as 15, but in the Western world usually begins at about 11. Thus girls tend to reach puberty ahead of boys. The age of onset has grown earlier this century as diets and living standards have improved. By 11 nipples (**a**) are becoming prominent and breasts (**b**), uterus (**c**), and ovaries (**d**) are growing. The pelvis broadens and pads of fat develop on the hips (**e**). Body hair (**f**) increases. Menstruation may begin between the ages of 11 and 13. Ovulation usually starts at about 14. Later, genitals mature and menstruation becomes more regular.

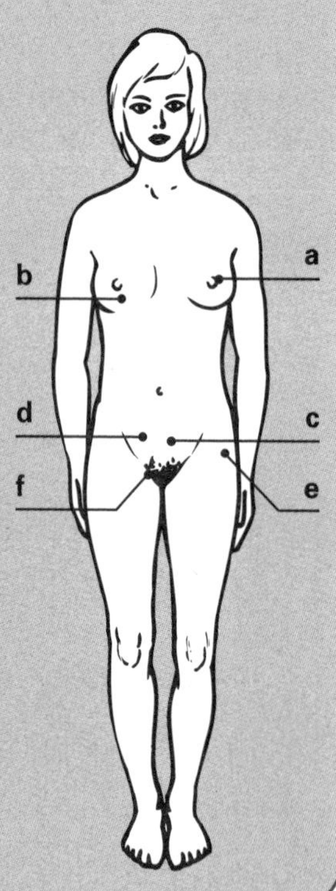

Chronic problems

Premenstrual problems

The body's overreaction to the hormonal changes triggered by the menstrual cycle produces premenstrual problems—notably premenstrual tension—in about half of all women. Discomfort sets in about a week before the menstrual flow starts, and stops when the flow begins.

On the left half of the illustration on the right common sites of problems, which are both physical and psychological, are shown.

1 Headaches (migraine sufferers report that they get their very worst headaches at this time).
2 Psychological tension, increasing feelings of nervousness and irritability.
3 Fatigue and depression.
4 Low backache.
5 Nausea.
6 Painful, tender, and swollen breasts.
7 Swollen feet and ankles produced by fluid collecting in the tissues. Thumb pressure drives it out, leaving the skin temporarily pitted.
8 Bloated abdomen (generally due to fluid retention).

The symptoms of premenstrual problems may be alleviated in several ways. Doctors may prescribe progesterone that modifies the hormonal changes of the menstrual cycle. A mild analgesic should help to stop discomfort, and limiting salt intake some days before menstruation helps to reduce tension. Drinking more water and hot herbal teas raises urine output and reduces fluid retention.

Menstrual problems
The right half of the illustration shows sites of major menstrual problems.

Lack of menstruation may be caused by:
9 Abnormality of the uterus.
10 Failure of the ovaries to stimulate the adolescent uterus, perhaps through malfunction of the hypothalamus gland.
11 The eating disorder called anorexia nervosa.
12 Malfunction of the pituitary gland: overproduction of prolactin, interfering with another hormone in the ovaries.

Irregular periods may be caused by:
13 A malfunction of the hypothalamus.

Painful periods may indicate:
14 Normal hormonal changes that affect the uterine muscle.
15 Pelvic damage caused by inflammation of the ovaries, fallopian tubes, and uterus, sometimes following abortion or childbirth. These internal organs may become "glued" to bowel or pelvic walls.
16 Similar damage caused by endometriosis, gonorrhea, or syphilis.

Heavy periods may suggest:
17 A troublesome intrauterine contraceptive device.
18 Some type of tumor, most notably (benign) uterine fibroids.

Postmenopausal bleeding has many possible causes. The most common are:
19 Cervical cancer.
20 Endometrial cancer.
21 Estrogen medication.

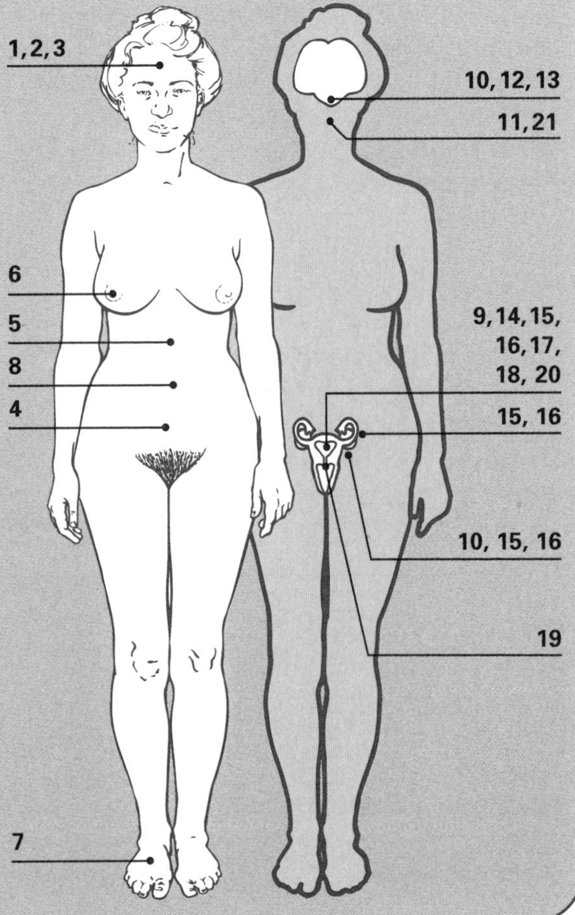

© DIAGRAM

Menstrual problems 2

Menstruation guidance

Do

- Prepare girls for the onset of menstruation—otherwise their first flow of blood can be frightening.
- See a doctor if menstruation has not started by the age of 16.
- Try a mild analgesic painkiller for acute premenstrual discomfort.
- Cut down the intake of salt or try a salt substitute for some days before menstruation starts.
- Exercise: this helps to reduce the discomfort that many women feel while menstruating.
- Seek medical help if you suffer severe period pains, especially one-sided, lower abdominal pain.
- Take extra iron in your diet if menstruation makes you anemic.
- Avoid constipation (exercise and bran in the diet help); it may worsen period pains.
- Get plenty of sleep and nourishing food to help to minimize period pains.
- See your doctor if you bleed very heavily, or bleed between periods or after menopause.

Don't

- Ignore severe premenstrual symptoms.
- Drink more liquids than usual in the few days before each period begins.
- Automatically cope with period pains by "giving up" (i.e. just taking time off work or going to bed).
- Become dependent on analgesics or tranquilizers to help you cope with premenstrual tension and period pains.
- Lead a life that lacks any regular vigorous exercise.
- Allow yourself to become constipated.
- Ignore heavy, irregular, or postmenopausal bleeding episodes, or more than a few months of missed periods. The longer you leave it the more difficult it may become to treat the underlying cause.

Absence of periods

Absence of menstruation is called amenorrhea. Girls who have never menstruated by 16 may have uterus or ovary problems requiring medical help. Women who stop having periods before menopause (average onset: 48) may be pregnant or breastfeeding a young baby. But amenorrhea is also linked with poor health, drug abuse, traveling, and emotional stress including fear, shock, depression, or tension, especially when there is loss of appetite and weight. Amenorrhea is often treatable with drugs that rebalance hormones.

Irregular periods

At certain times in life it is quite common for menstruation to be irregular. In the first months after menarche a girl may miss one or two periods (but if she has had intercourse she should test for pregnancy).

Even adult women may find that their menstrual cycle may be as short as 21 days or as long as 35. However, disorders of the hypothalamus in the base of the brain can cause periods to become irregular.

Heavy and light periods

Most women shed between two and four tablespoons of blood during each period. Some lose more, some less. At menarche, the discharge may redden only gradually. Women using contraceptive pills have light periods, and periods change as menopause approaches. Prolonged bleeding may occur at menarche, or with intrauterine contraceptive devices. Heavy bleeding may also occur for psychological reasons.

Painful periods

Dysmenorrhea (painful periods) may be primary or acquired. Primary dysmenorrhea is due to hormonal changes; it may cause a day's discomfort or cramping pain in the lower abdomen with nausea and headaches. It is often worst in tense people. Taking exercise helps, and doctors may prescribe analgesics, iron supplements, and contraceptive pills. Acquired dysmenorrhea is due to disease and features one-sided pain. Surgery may be needed.

Exercising

Doctors believe there is a close link between exercise and lack of period pains. They point out that healthy, active women and girls suffer least, and some athletes claim they feel fittest while menstruating. On the other hand many women suffering period pains perform sedentary work. This encourages constipation, which is a factor that helps to promote dysmenorrhea. Leaving school to take up a sedentary job often coincides with the onset of painful periods, at least partly because the individual may stop sports activities. Instead of taking to your bed with hot blankets and analgesics to relieve mild pains, many doctors suggest eating an iron-enriched diet (to combat loss of iron in menstruation) and exercise. The following types of exercise are among those considered suitable. Walking: this should be brisk and done for a fairly extended period. It provides rhythmic exercise yet does not strain individual joints. Swimming: this is a fine all-around activity, exercising the heart, lungs, and muscles, and helping to keep joints flexible. Cycling: riding provides useful exercise, although some people complain it accentuates back problems. Dancing: this is helpful if it is vigorous.

© DIAGRAM

Female system disorders

Inside the female reproductive system, ovaries produce eggs and the female sex hormones estrogen and progesterone. A ripe egg from an ovary passes through a fallopian tube to the uterus. Meanwhile a penis inserted into the vagina will ejaculate sperm-containing semen. The sperm cells travel up through the cervix, and then through the uterus, to fertilize the egg. The fertilized egg travels down the fallopian tube and becomes implanted in the uterine wall until it has grown into a full-term baby, and is forced by contractions through the vagina and out of the mother's body. Sexual (or other types of) infection can affect all parts of the female genital tract, and some parts are liable to damage or displacement. Some ailments are merely irritating, but others can cause infertility or chronic illness, and occasionally even death if not diagnosed and treated promptly enough.

Female reproductive problems

1 Ovarian cysts are sacs of mucus or fluid that grow in the egg-shaped ovaries, and which may be tiny or large enough to cause visible swelling. Some cysts become twisted, producing sudden severe pain, nausea, and even life-threatening shock reactions; troublesome or large cysts need to be drained or removed surgically.

2 Solid ovarian tumors may be benign or malignant. Some tumors produce female hormones, causing precocious sexual development in young girls or postmenopausal bleeding. A few tumors produce male hormones, which deepen the voice, shrink the breasts, and produce facial hair.

3 Salpingitis is inflammation of the fallopian tubes caused by bacterial infection, most frequently gonorrhea. Pain often occurs in the lower abdomen with cervical discharge; infertility and peritonitis (an infection of the lining of the body cavity) may be complications if the condition is left untreated.

4 The uterus in a non-pregnant woman is a small, pear-shaped organ; during pregnancy the fertilized egg embeds itself in the endometrium (the blood-rich lining of the uterus), and the uterus enlarges to make room for the developing fetus.

5 Endometriosis is the abnormal growth of endometrial cells outside the uterus, lining the fallopian tubes, ovaries, and nonsexual organs in the pelvic region. This causes backache and abdominal pain, particularly at menstruation.

6 Fibroids are benign tumors of the uterus. They are present in 20 percent of women aged 35 to 40 and range from the size of a pinhead to the size of an unborn baby. Large fibroids disturb normal menstruation and bladder action, and require surgical removal.

7 The uterus is generally folded forward when a woman is not pregnant. Occasionally it becomes tilted backward or drops downward in some women. This causes discomfort, increases the likelihood of infections and problems with urination.

8 Cervicitis is the inflammation of the cervix—the neck of the uterus. Cervicitis is caused by bacterial or fungal infection and produces thin, clear mucus, perhaps streaked with blood or pus.

9 Cervical erosion is a rough, reddened area lining the os (cervical opening) that requires electric cauterization if it causes persistent trouble.

10 Cervical polyps are benign tumors in the cervix linked to warts; sometimes producing bleeding, discharge, pain, and infertility. They should be removed surgically.

11 Vaginitis is inflammation of the vagina, the muscular passage between the cervix and the external genitals.

12 Vulvitis is inflammation of the vulva, the external female genitals.

13 Syphilitic sores and other venereal lesions may show up on the vulva.

14 Pubic skin troubles include sores, ulcers, warts, and mite and louse infestations—all resulting from sexual contact.

Cross section of female reproductive system

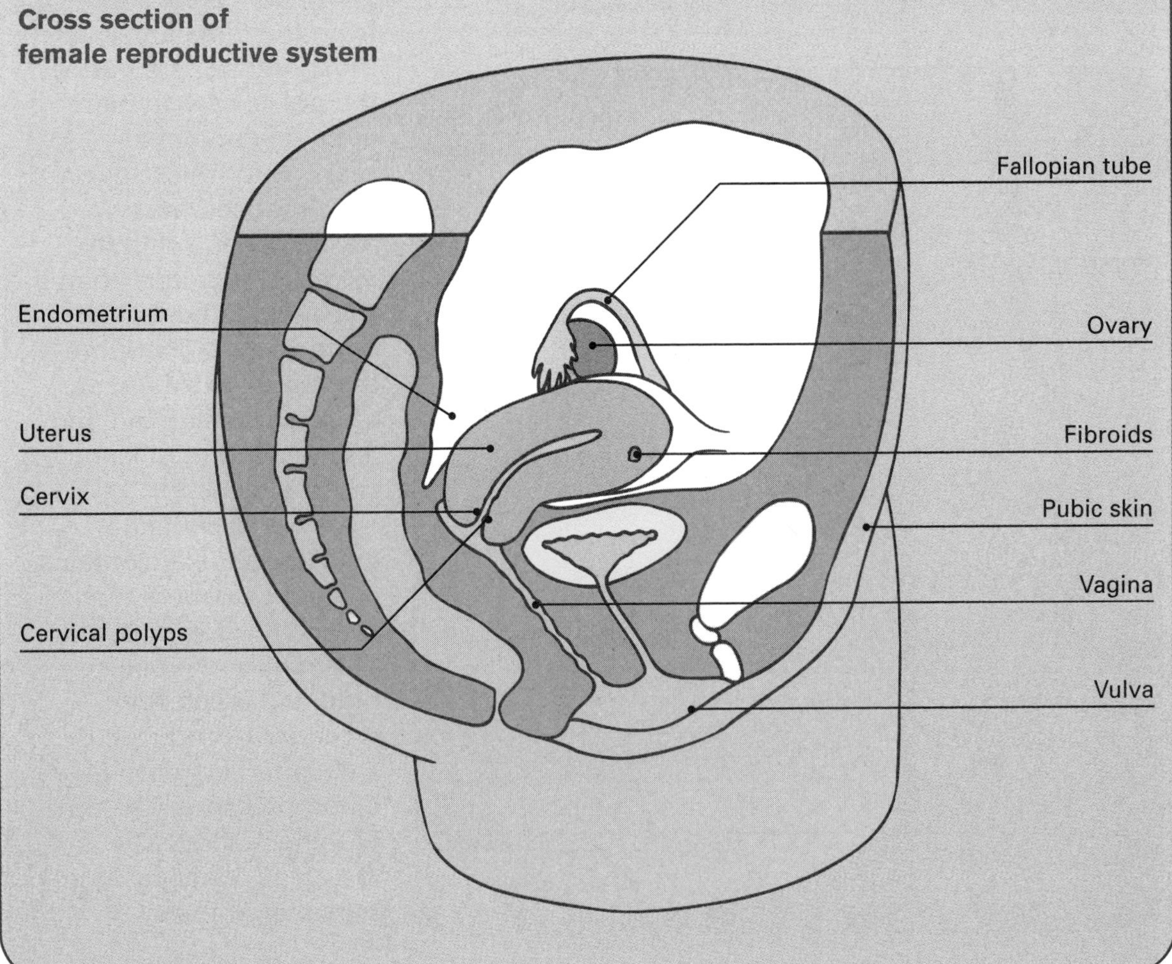

© DIAGRAM

The male reproductive system produces spermatozoa, or sperm cells, in the testes. These cells are then mixed with a nutrient-rich liquid to form semen. The semen is then ejaculated at high speed through the penis while it is inserted into a woman's vagina. The penis is mainly made of erectile tissue, like a female clitoris. It becomes erect when a man is sexually aroused. The erection makes it easier for the penis to enter the vagina and also helps to stimulate the woman sexually.

Temperature-sensitive

- The exposed location of the testes means that they are at a temperature about 3°F (1.3°C) lower than normal body temperature. This is essential for sperm survival.

Male genital organs

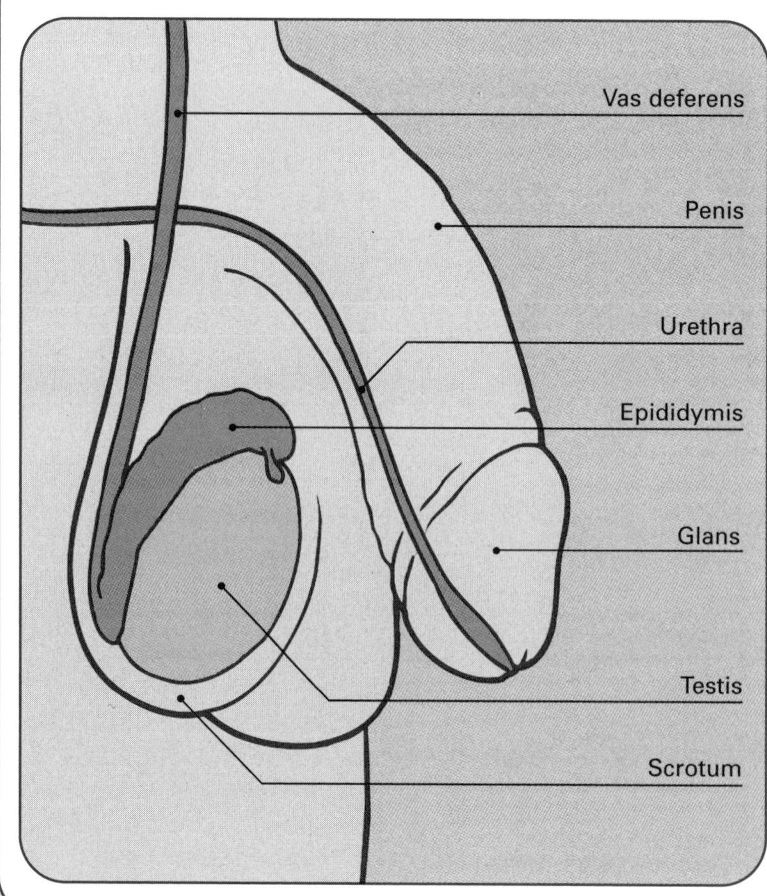

External genitals

The male genitals differ from the female because most of them are outside the pelvic cavity. There are a few potential reasons for this. Sperm are produced most efficiently at a slightly lower temperature than the average body temperature. Therefore the testes (male gonads) are kept outside the body in the scrotum to keep them cooler.

The penis contains erectile tissue. It contains several chambers that can be filled with blood. This makes the penis rigid and erect. An erection is produced by a localized increase in blood pressure. The tip of the erectile tissue is the glans, which is highly sensitive to touch.

Male reproductive system

Structure	Functions
Seminal vesicles	• Produce the semen (or seminal fluid) in which sperm (male sex cells) leave the body.
Prostate gland	• Secretes fluid that helps activate sperm during ejaculation.
Vas deferens	• Moves sperm from epididymis to urethra using muscular wave movements.
Cowper's gland	• Secretions form part of seminal fluid.
Urethra	• Carries sperm and seminal fluid to the penis tip during ejaculation; and • carries urine from the bladder during urination.
Penis	• Delivers sperm outside the body (in particular, to the female reproductive organs during sexual intercourse); and • is involved in male sexual response.
Epididymis	• Stores sperm cells while they mature.
Testes	• Produce sperm cells and male sex hormones (regulatory chemicals) including testosterone.
Scrotum	• Contains the testes and keeps them cooler than the rest of the body, which is necessary for efficient sperm production.

Median section through male pelvis

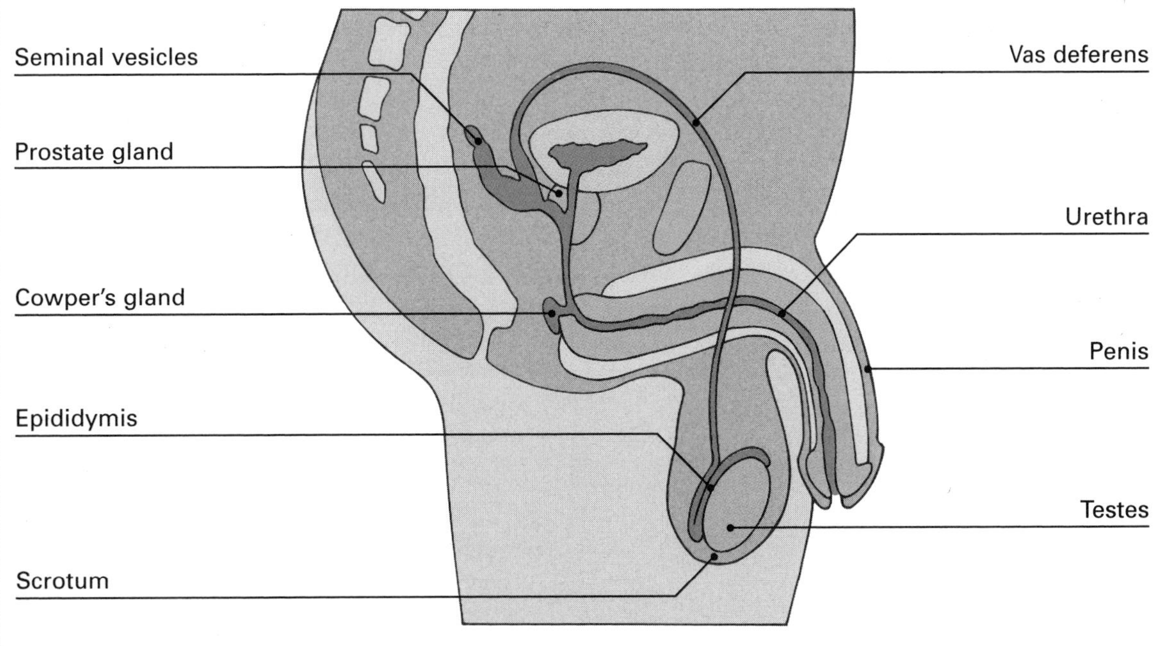

© DIAGRAM

Internal male genitals

The male genitals are closely associated with the excretory system, which includes the kidneys and bladder (which holds urine and is drained through the urethra in the penis). Consequently the genitals are often described as part of the urinogenital (or urogenital) system.

Each testis forms, along with its epididymis, a testicle. Normally there are two testicles inside the scrotum, although some men have just one.

Both of the testicles are linked to the outside of the body by a system of ducts. The matured sperm leave the epididymis and travel along the vas deferentia to the prostate gland. Inside this donut-shaped gland the sperm cells are mixed with fluids and nutrients that make up semen. The seminal fluids activate the sperm before it is forced out along the urethra by contractions of the glands. This is called ejaculation.

Front view of the male reproductive tract

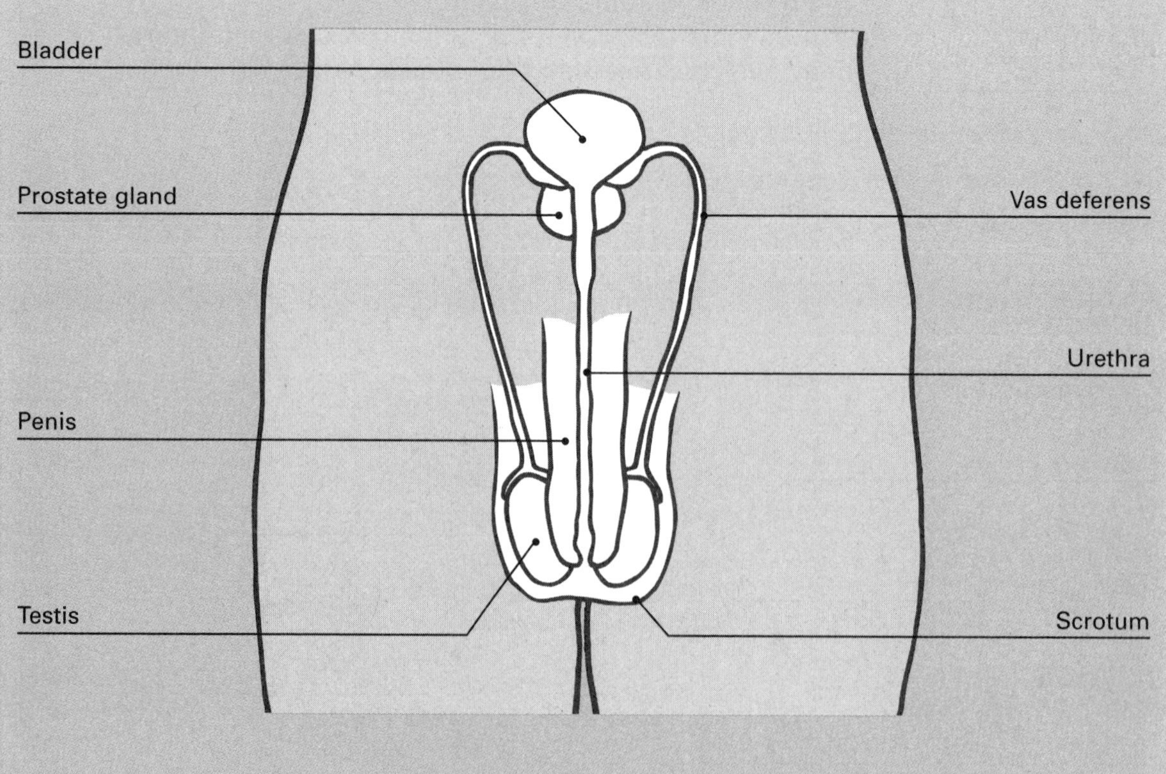

Genital blood supply

The male genitals are supplied with blood in the same way as the female system. The blood supply for both testicles arrives directly from the aorta, the main artery coming directly from the heart. The left testicle's blood drains into the left renal vein, which serves the left kidney, while the right testicle's vein joins directly to the vena cava, the body's main vein.

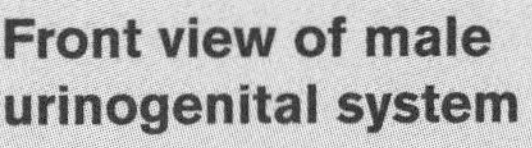

Front view of male urinogenital system

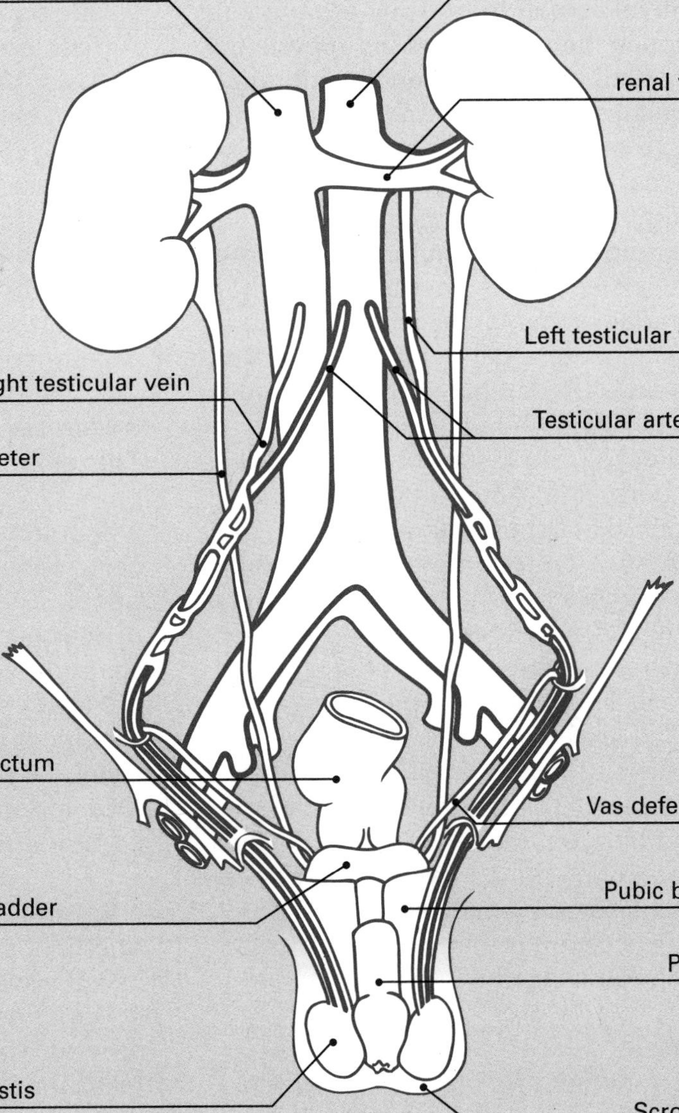

Inferior vena cava
Aorta
Left renal vein
Left testicular vein
Right testicular vein
Testicular arteries
Ureter
Rectum
Vas deferens
Pubic bone
Bladder
Penis
Testis
Scrotum

Lower gonads

- The male gonads descend into the scrotum during fetal development, so the blood vessels that serve them have to be a little longer than their female counterparts.

© DIAGRAM

Production of sperm

The formation of sperm

Male gametes (sex cells) are commonly known as sperm. "Sperm" is actually short for spermatozoon (plural: spermatozoa). Spermatozoa are relatively small cells. They are unusual because they can move independently, propelled by tail-like flagella (singular: flagellum). Just like female gametes, sperm differ from somatic cells (those in the rest of the body) in that they contain half a full set of chromosomes. (Chromosomes are cellular structures that carry genes—inherited genetic material.) When a sperm fuses with a female gamete (an ovum) their half-sets of genes are combined to make a full set, which is unique. Gametes are produced from a set of body cells called the germ line. Any mutations (genetic errors) that occur in the germ line may be passed on to the next generation. The process by which male gametes are formed is known as spermatogenesis. It involves two types of cell division: mitosis and meiosis. Spermatogenesis begins around the age of 14 and continues throughout life. Pubescent boys may be able to ejaculate before spermatogenesis has started, but their semen does not contain viable sex cells. It takes several weeks for a spermatozoon to be formed and reach full maturity.

1 Inside the testes

Spermatogenesis takes place within seminiferous tubules (coiled tubes) inside the testes. The seminiferous tubules are lined with immature cells called spermatogonia or stem cells. Each stem cell has 46 chromosomes. This is a full set for a normal human being.

2 Mitosis

At first, spermatogonia multiply by mitosis. Mitosis is the most common type of cell division. It involves a cell splitting into two daughter cells, each of which are genetically identical, that is, they contain the same set of genes. Each of the cells produced by mitosis of spermatogonia are called primary spermatocytes. These still have 46 chromosomes.

3 Meiosis

This cell division is used to make gametes only. It involves two divisions, which together produce four daughter cells, each with a unique half set of genes. The first meiotic division of a primary spermatocyte produces two secondary spermatocytes. These cells have 23 chromosomes each. The second meiotic division splits these two secondary spermatocytes into a total of four spermatids, still with 23 chromosomes in each cell.

4 Spermiogenesis

The final stage of spermatogenesis is called spermiogenesis. It occurs when spermatids mature into spermatozoa (or sperm). The final maturation process takes place in the epididymides above the testes. The entire spermatogenesis process takes about 90 days.

The process of spermatogenesis

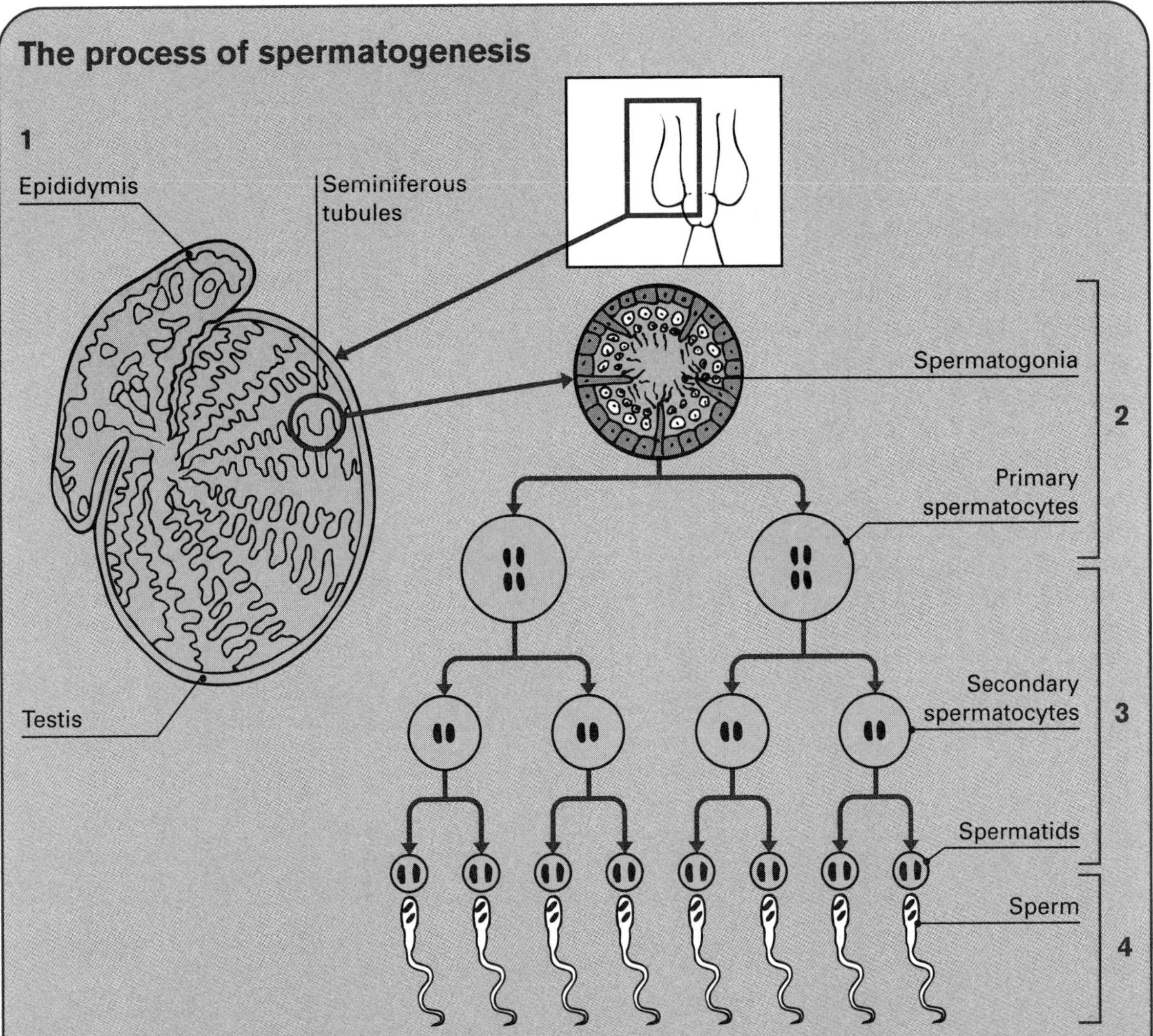

Gametes

Ova (female sex cells, also known as eggs) and spermatozoa (male sex cells, also known as sperm) are collectively called gametes. Human body cells have 46 chromosomes (structures that carry inherited material). Gametes differ from other body cells in that they only have 23 chromosomes. This ensures that when a sperm and ova fuse together the resulting fertilized cell has 46 chromosomes and no more.

© DIAGRAM

Testes

The scrotum

The scrotum is made up of several layers. The outer layer is a covering of loose skin. Inside this is the dartos muscle, which contracts to wrinkle the scrotal skin. Beneath the dartos layer is the cremaster muscle. This muscle contracts to pull the testicle up. This is done chiefly when the testes are too cold. The next layer is the tunica vaginalis or vaginal tunic. This covers the testis and epididymis.

Section through the layers of the scrotum

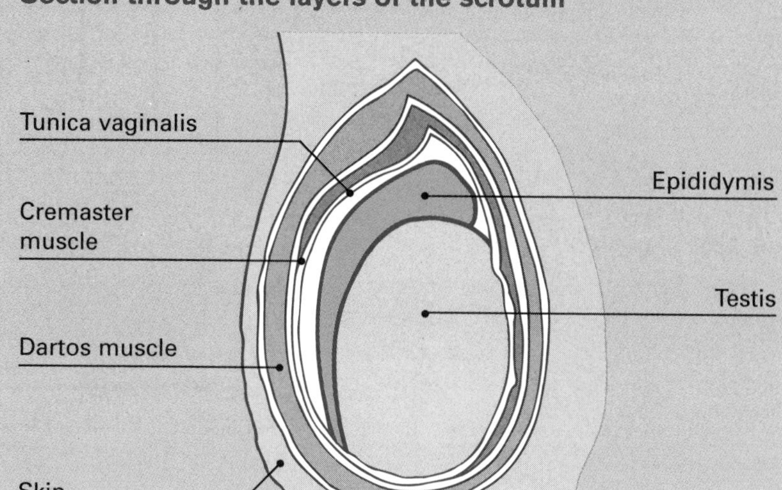

Internal structure

The testicle is connected to the rest of the reproductive system via the spermatic cord. This holds the vas deferens, artery, vein, and nerves. Inside the tunica vaginalis is a white tissue called the tunica albuginea, which covers the lobules of the testis. These lobules are separated by septula. The fold of skin at the join between the scrotum's two testicles is called the septum.

Section through testis and epididymis

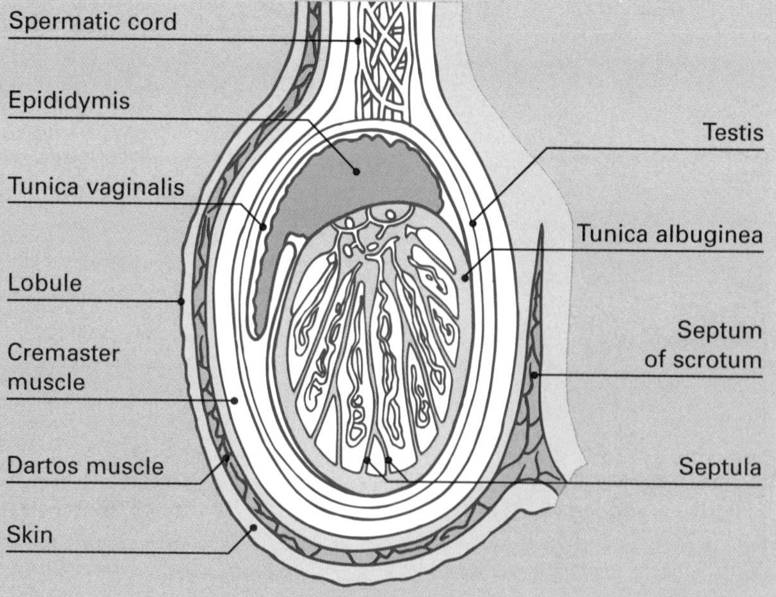

Inside the testis

Each lobule of the testis is filled with seminiferous tubules. These are lined with spermatogonia which divide into spermatocytes. These build up toward the center of the tubule. In the middle of the tubule maturing spermatozoa are found. These travel along the tubules through the testis to the epididymis. There the sperm are stored for about 10 days until they are mature.

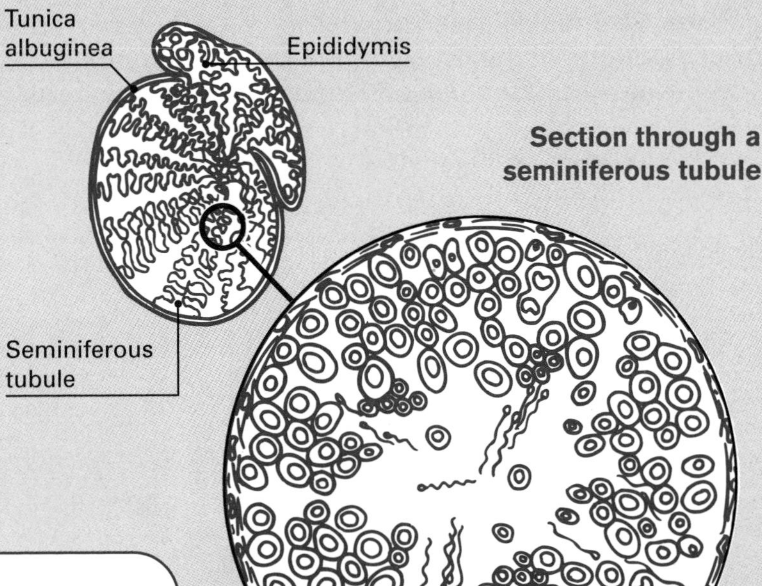

Sperm maturation

Male gametes do not begin to develop their flagella until they become spermatids. Mature sperm are about 0.002 inches (55 μm) long.

Stages in maturation of spermatazoa

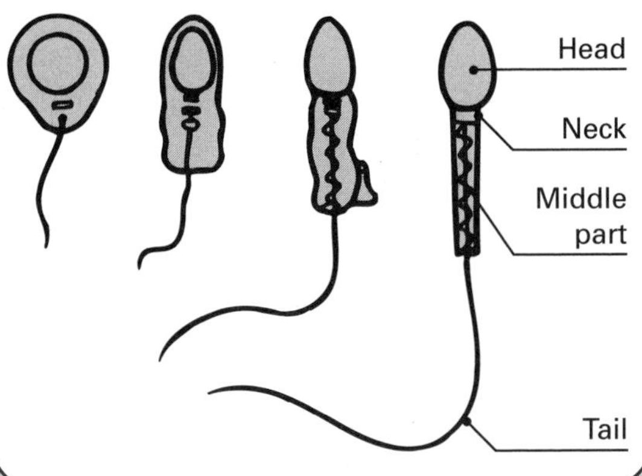

Sperm facts

- A healthy adult male produces about 200 million sperm every day.
- The volume of ejaculated semen is generally between from 0.07 to 0.2 fluid ounce (2 to 6 ml). Each milliliter of semen contains 100 million sperm.
- Although male humans do not undergo menopause like females, sperm production does begin to drop at the age of 45.

© DIAGRAM

Penis

Inside the penis

The penis is the outlet for both urine from the bladder and sperm from the gonads. Both fluids travel down the urethra, a tube at the center of the penis. The fleshy part of the penis is made up of three shafts of erectile tissue: two cavernous bodies (corpora cavernosa) and one spongy body (corpus spongiosum). The urethra passes through the spongy body.

Section through the male urethra as seen from above

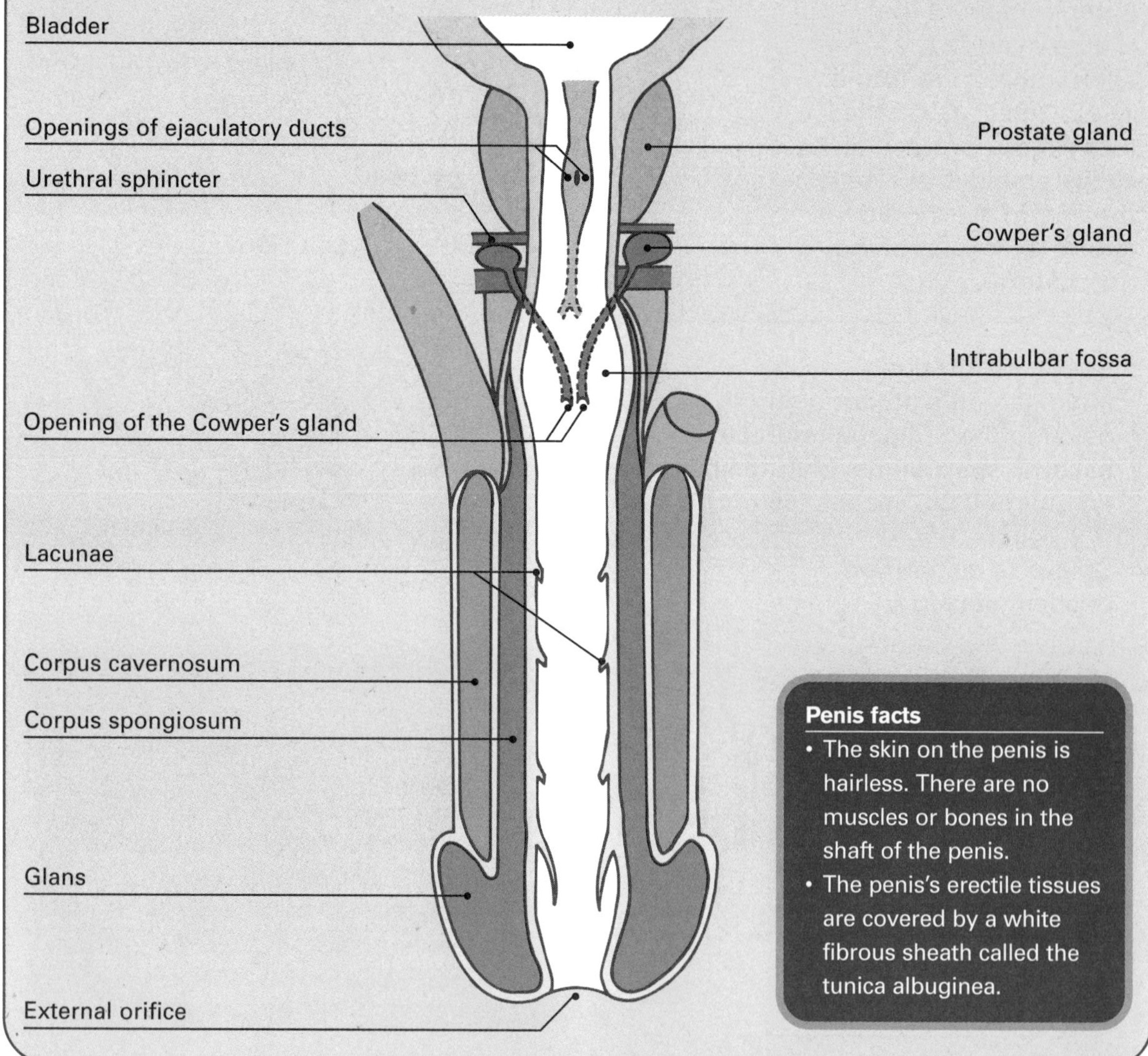

Penis facts

- The skin on the penis is hairless. There are no muscles or bones in the shaft of the penis.
- The penis's erectile tissues are covered by a white fibrous sheath called the tunica albuginea.

Erectile tissue

The corpora cavernosa and corpus spongiosum are erectile tissue. The two corpora cavernosa are divided by part of the tunica albuginea called the septum. The tip of the corpus spongiosum expands into the glans. This is covered by the foreskin, which is attached to the frenulum. The erectile tissue is filled with hollow caverns, or lacunae, which fill with blood during erection.

Cross section through shaft

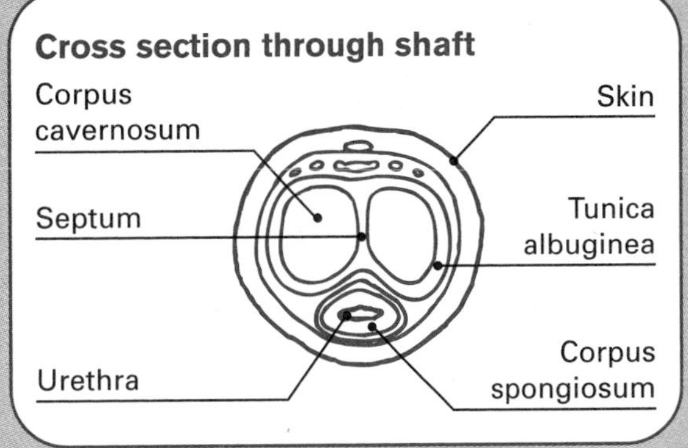

Erectile bodies and muscles

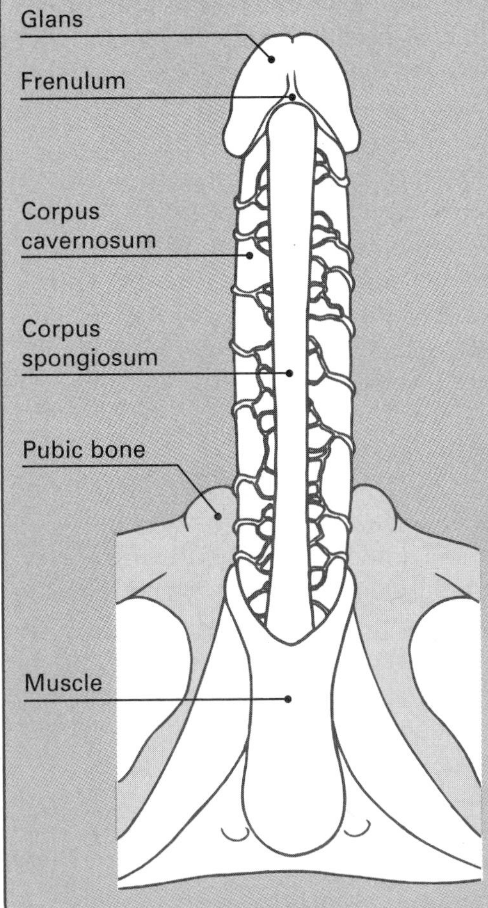

Longitudinal section seen from above

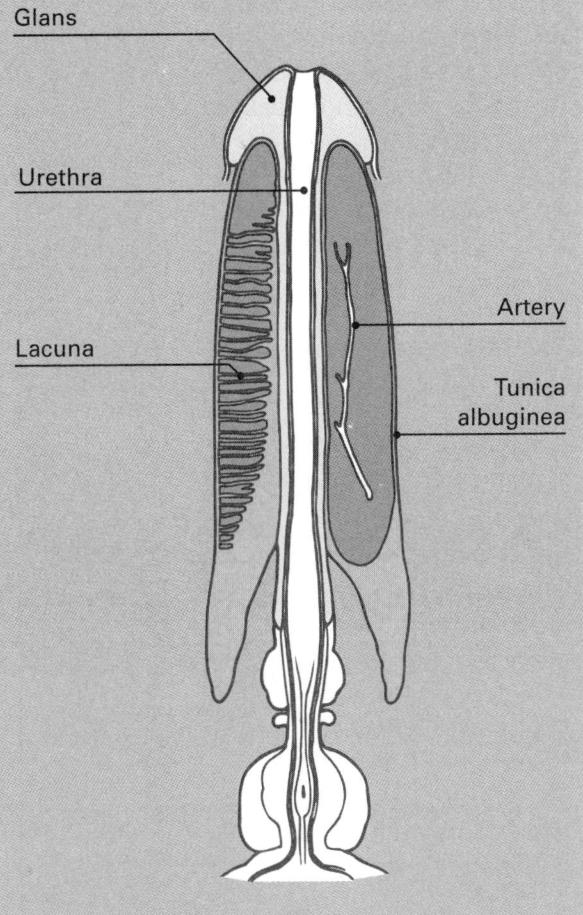

© DIAGRAM

The main male sex organs are the penis and two bean-shaped testes suspended in the scrotal sac, visible below the base of the penis. Testes produce the male hormone testosterone, and sperm for fertilizing a woman's ova. Tubes carry sperm through the reproductive tract, where glands lubricate and nourish them. At orgasm muscular contractions force the resulting semen (a sticky white fluid) through the urethra and from the tip of the penis, which is then stiff and hard. The main problems afflicting the male reproductive system are infections, congenital malformations, and benign and malignant prostate gland conditions. Most sexual conditions can be helped and anyone with a reproductive system problem should see a doctor.

Onset of puberty

This varies from boy to boy but usually starts about age 12, soon after the so-called adolescent growth spurt has set in. By age 12 the testes (**a**) are growing noticeably (two years earlier they are only a fraction of their adult size). Between the age of 12 and 15 the penis (**b**) starts to grow and undergoes spontaneous erection more often than before. Pubic hair (**c**) begins to grow around the base of the penis and the testes begin secreting immature sperm, with nocturnal emission possible. The prostate gland (**d**) grows. Between the ages of 15 and 18, mature sperm are produced and pubic hair coarsens.

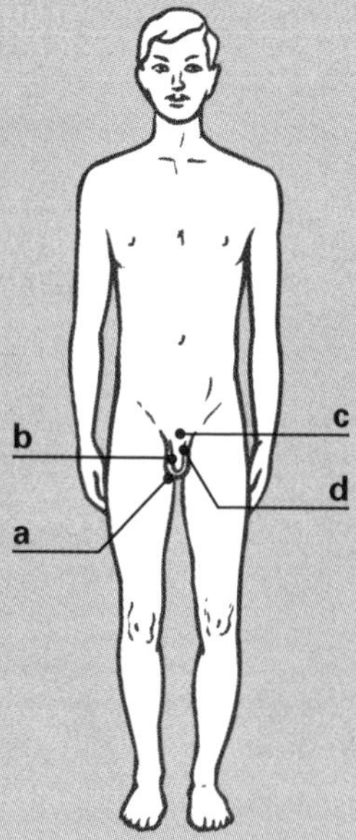

Prostate problems

Prostatitis is inflammation of the prostate gland, due to urinary tract infection, and occurs in younger men. There may be pain, local tenderness, and difficulty passing urine. The acutely ill need bed rest, antibiotics, analgesics, and eight to ten glasses of water daily. Weekly prostatic massage for six to eight weeks may help. Avoid alcohol and sex. Benign prostate enlargement occurs mainly in men over 60. It may be symptomless. But if you pass urine little and often, with difficulty or discomfort, and your stools are very thin, you may need surgery. Cancer of the prostate has similar symptoms and requires surgery or hormone treatment.

Hygiene

Poor penis hygiene encourages accumulations of white smegma under the foreskin in uncircumcised men, causing inflammation of the foreskin and penis tip with an offensive discharge. Accumulating smegma is also linked with certain cancers in men and in women with whom they have intercourse. Good penis hygiene stops smegma from collecting and so prevents such troubles. Uncircumcised males should take care to wash beneath the foreskin regularly. To do this they should first retract the foreskin; if inflammation prevents this, a doctor may prescribe ointment to clear up the infection.

Hydrocele

This is a soft swelling in the scrotum, produced by a larger than normal accumulation of the fluid that helps protect the testes and leaves them free to move about. One side or both sides of the scrotal sac may be affected. A hydrocele is present in many newborn male babies and the condition usually corrects itself within the first two years of life. But if a loop of intestine herniates down into the scrotum through a channel, this may also fill with fluid, producing swelling in both the groin and scrotum. If this happens surgery is required. Any swelling in the scrotum or groin should be investigated by a doctor.

Circumcision

This practice involves removing the foreskin, a loose fold of skin that covers the glans of the penis near its tip. Circumcision is a religious requirement for Jews and Muslims. This operation has the practical benefit of preventing the build-up of smegma beneath the foreskin. However, circumcised babies are liable to get ulcers at the penis tip. As a man ages, the skin in the glans may harden and become less sensitive. Provided males maintain good penis hygiene there is no medical reason for routine circumcision; rare emergency circumcision may be required if the foreskin swells and blocks the urethral outlet.

Undescended testes

Testes develop in the abdomen and normally descend into the scrotum about eight weeks before birth. Sometimes they are only in the groin by birth but fall soon afterward. Even normally descended testes temporarily rise into the groin. If in any doubt whether testes have descended examine the baby after a warm bath, but avoid handling the testes. If both have not descended by the age of two a doctor may advise surgery if only one testis is involved, or hormonal drugs if both are undescended. Patients must be treated before puberty. Otherwise, testes and sperm may not develop properly, causing infertility and a risk of cancer.

Inguinal hernia

An inguinal hernia occurs when part of the intestine bulges down into the inguinal canal—the channel through which, in men, the testes drop into the scrotum before birth. Because this canal is larger in men than in women, more males suffer inguinal hernias than females. In men, inguinal hernia results from weak inguinal muscles; in boys it may be linked with a small developmental defect. A hernial sac may disappear while the patient lies down if the intestine slips back into the abdomen. Inguinal hernias are usually corrected by surgery to avoid the severe complications that may arise if they are left untreated.

© DIAGRAM

Male system disorders

The main problems afflicting the male reproductive system are infections, congenital malformations, and benign and malignant prostate gland conditions. Problems can arise in any part of the system. Infections and other problems involving the kidneys, bladder, and intestines can impact the genitals. Most health problems with the sexual organs can be treated. Some can cause serious problems or even be fatal, so anyone with a worrying condition should see a doctor.

Male reproductive system and its problems

The two testes hang below the body in the scrotum where they are cool enough to produce fertile sperm. Testes secrete testosterone, a hormone producing male sex characteristics.

1 Testes that remain inside the abdomen fail to produce fertile sperm, and may also develop cancer.

2 Scrotal swelling may result from accumulated fluid, hernias, cysts, or tumors.

3 Inflammation of testes (orchitis) is usually due to mumps but can be caused by gonorrhea. Either way the consequence may be infertility, although this is a rare complication of mumps.

4 Varicose veins around the scrotum produce the condition varicocele, sometimes causing infertility. Regularly bathing the testes in cold water may help, or veins can be removed.

5 Billions of tiny, tadpole-like sperm cells develop in tiny tubes inside the testes each month. But if a high proportion is misshapen or lacks mobility, the producer may be infertile.

6 Epididymides are convoluted tubes at the top and rear of each testis. They store maturing sperm until these are ejaculated or disintegrate. In gonorrhea, epididymides may grow inflamed and become painful.

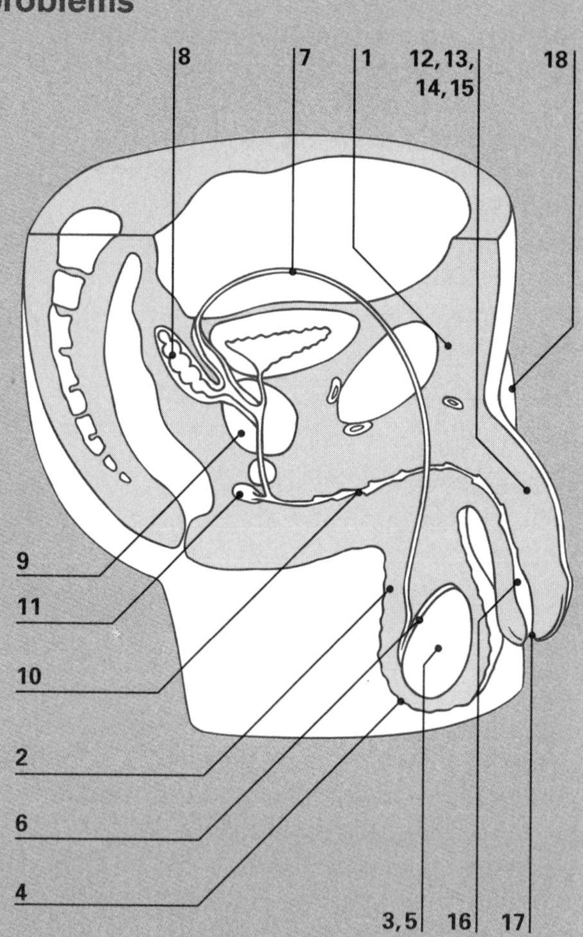

7 The vas deferens tubes take sperm from the epididymides to the seminal vesicles. Tubal blockage by venereal diseases can cause infertility, though this can be treated by bypass surgery.

8 Seminal vesicles store sperm and secrete fluid for it. They seldom get infected.
9 The prostate gland produces fluid to feed and stimulate sperm. It is liable to suffer inflammation or enlargement. This will also cause problems with urination.
10 The urethra carries sperm and urine from the body. It sometimes suffers inflammation or blockage due to infection or kidney stones.
11 Cowper's gland adds lubricating fluid to semen. It is rarely infected.
12 The penis encloses the outer end of the urethra. When erect, the penis can be inserted into a vagina.
13 Congenital penis problems include a misplaced urethral outlet.
14 Acquired penis deformations include crooked erection due to injury; and nonsexual erection (priapism) with various possible causes.
15 Inability to achieve an erection may occur from psychological or physical causes.
16 A painful penis may be due to inflammation or obstruction elsewhere in the urinary tract.
17 Some sexual infections show as sores on, or discharge from, the tip of the penis.
18 Pubic skin troubles include sores, ulcers, warts, and mite and louse infestations—all resulting from sexual contact.

Impotence

This means being unable to gain or maintain an erection and so have sexual intercourse. Many men are impotent at some time. Nine-tenths of cases are due to fear of failure, dislike of sex, or other psychological causes. Most temporary bouts of impotence can be cured by the restoration of good communication between the partners, so that misunderstandings, fears, and unreal expectations can be removed; if the man has a warm, loving, and understanding partner his confidence, and potency, will soon return. Cases of long-term impotence may need psychological counseling, and many respond to therapy.

Urethritis

As its name implies, urethritis involves inflammation of the urethra. There may be discharge from the penis and urination can be painful. If untreated, the prostate, bladder, and testes may all become involved, with local pain and swelling. The cause may be gonorrhea, or bacteria invading the urinary system. Nonspecific urethritis (the most common type) can be due to unidentified germs or a reaction to chemicals in the vagina of the sexual partner. Patients should drink eight to ten glasses of water daily. Analgesics may relieve pain, and antibiotics kill most kinds of urethritis-causing germs.

© DIAGRAM

Pregnancy is the period from conception (when a sperm and ovum fuse at fertilization) to the birth of the baby. During this time, the zygote (the single cell produced by the fusion of sperm and ovum) changes into an embryo and then, after eight weeks, a fetus. Pregnancy, also called gestation, lasts for about 40 weeks in humans. During this time the uterus expands many times over to make room for the growing baby. The word "pregnancy" is derived from the Middle English for "before birth."

Pregnancy facts

- The average time it takes for a couple to achieve a pregnancy is six months.
- Embryos produce human chorionic gonadotrophin (HCG). This is detected by pregnancy tests.

Stages in pregnancy

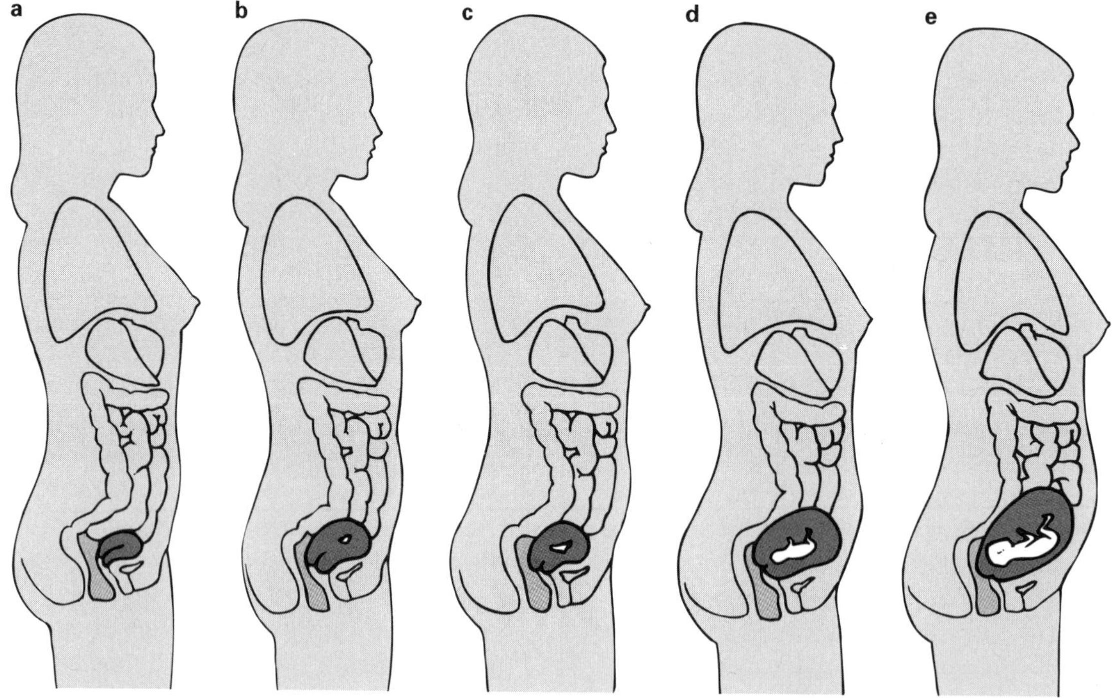

a Four weeks: The zygote has developed into a ball of cells called a blastocyst. Near the end of the month, the blastocyst is implanted into the uterus's endometrium.

b Eight weeks: The major organs begin to develop from three distinct layers of cells in the fetus.

c 12 weeks: The fetus has well-developed eyes, genitals, and heart.

d 16 weeks: The fetus's body parts are now all in place. It can hear. Fine hairs appear on the body.

e 20 weeks: The fetus's muscles develop and its movements increase.

Signs of pregnancy

In most cases the first sign of a possible pregnancy is the lack of a period at the expected time. Soon after this, and sometimes before, a woman may start to feel sick owing to large changes in hormone levels. This may be worse in the morning but may occur at any time. Other signs include a metallic taste in the mouth; tiredness and dizzy spells; changes in the breasts, such as tingles and tenderness; food cravings; and mood swings.

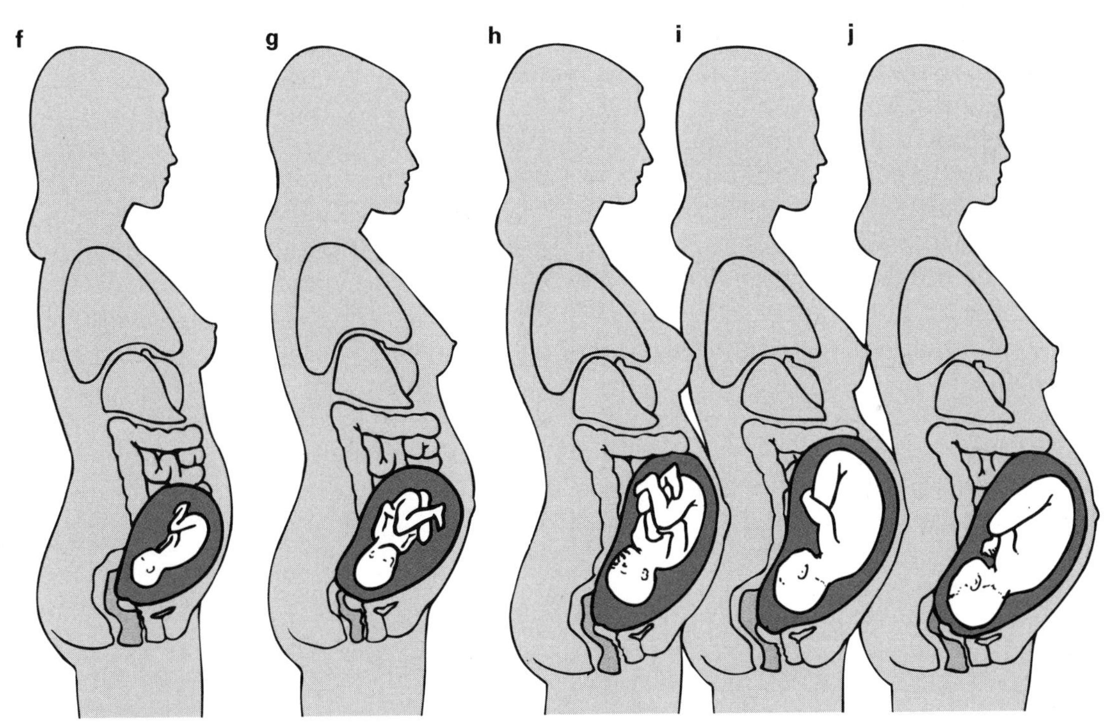

f 24 weeks: The fetus follows a pattern of sleep and wakefulness.
g 28 weeks: Fat deposits build up in the fetus's body. Waxy vernix waterproofs the skin inside the fluid-filled uterus.
h 32 weeks: The baby's head moves down to the cervix in preparation for birth.
i 36 weeks: The fetus puts on weight and has hair and fingernails.
j 40 weeks: The baby is full size and is ready to be born.

© DIAGRAM

Overview of pregnancy

A full-term pregnancy lasts approximately 266 days. Since it is impossible to pinpoint exactly when conception occurred, pregnancies are timed from the last menstrual period. This is generally 14 days before conception becomes possible. Therefore the average pregnancy lasts 280 days, or 40 weeks. For convenience this time-span is divided into three equal parts, or trimesters. Each trimester presents its own particular concerns and problems for the mother as the baby within her develops and her body changes to accommodate it. As well as the physical changes during pregnancy, the expectant mother has to adapt her routine and her family life to prepare for the birth and homecoming of the baby. The mother's life will be altered radically, particularly with a first baby, and much of the advice given during pregnancy is designed to help her make this transition easily.

The first trimester

This period covers the first three months, or 13 weeks, of the pregnancy. By the fourth week, illustrated below, the fertilized egg is established in the uterus, and the embryo is forming, but the uterus has not yet started to enlarge. Pregnancy can usually be confirmed at week five by a urine test and at week eight by an internal examination. Drugs, alcohol, and tobacco can affect the baby's development adversely in this trimester, and so should be avoided as much as possible. Morning sickness is common during this time, but usually disappears by the end of the trimester.

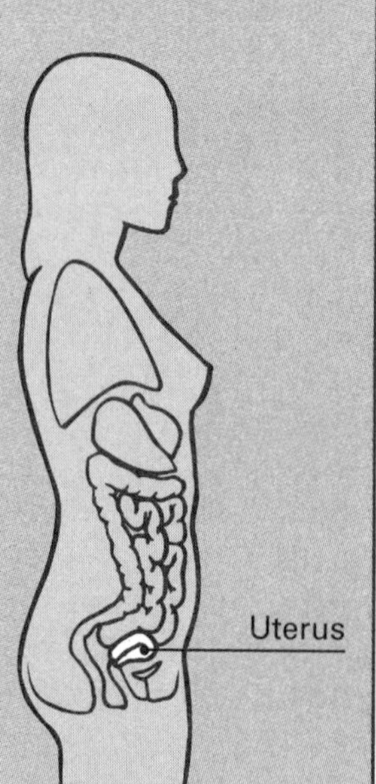

The second trimester

This period covers the second three months of the pregnancy, weeks 14 to 26. By week 16, illustrated below, the mother's abdomen has begun to swell visibly; by the end of the trimester the swelling will be very marked. Early in the trimester the fetal heart can be heard through a stethoscope; by the end of the trimester the fetus will be about 13 inches (33 cm) long. By that stage its eyes will be open and it will be moving about in the uterus. These movements can be felt by the mother. The mother may develop food cravings during this trimester, but these should be indulged only if they are nutritious.

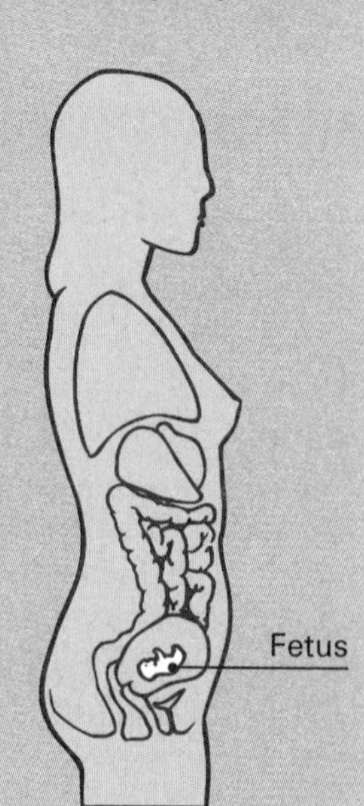

Danger signs

If any of these symptoms occur, a doctor should be seen immediately.

- Continuous headache.
- Frequent fainting.
- Blurred vision.
- Excessive vomiting.
- Severe abdominal pain.
- No fetal movements for two days in late pregnancy.
- Release of amniotic fluid from the uterus (breaking of the waters).
- Vaginal bleeding, other than small amounts at the times of the first missed periods.
- Pain on urination.
- Bad swelling of the hands, face, or ankles.

The third trimester

This period covers the last three months of pregnancy, from week 27 to about week 40. At week 28, illustrated below, the fetus is legally regarded as capable of independent life; if born at this stage it has a five percent chance of survival. Babies born before week 38 and weighing less than 5 lbs., 8 oz. (2.5 kg) are termed premature, and often require special care. During this trimester the baby increases rapidly in size and weight, and the mother's posture changes as she adapts to the increased load. Her navel flattens, and heartburn often occurs as the stomach is pushed upward by the displaced diaphragm.

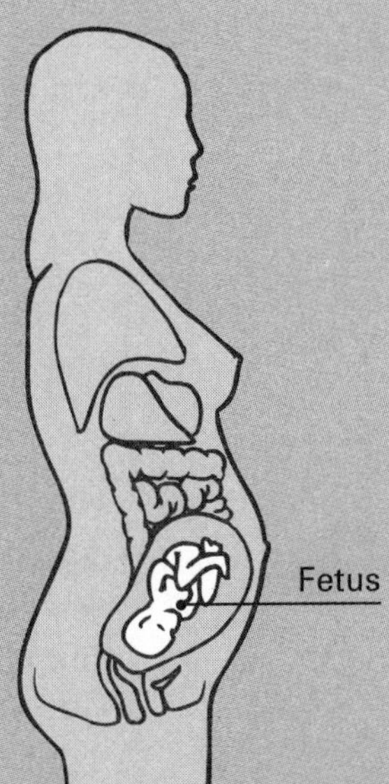

At birth

By week 40, illustrated below, the baby's head is engaged in the mother's pelvic cavity ready for birth. If the baby is not in the correct position, it can sometimes be turned by careful manipulation of the mother's abdomen. The baby is about 20 inches (50 kg) long and weighs on average 7 lbs., 8 oz. (3.4 kg). When the mother's body is ready to give birth, the uterus contracts rhythmically, producing labor pains. The early contractions soften and open the cervix, and later contractions push the baby out of the mother's body through the vagina, or birth canal.

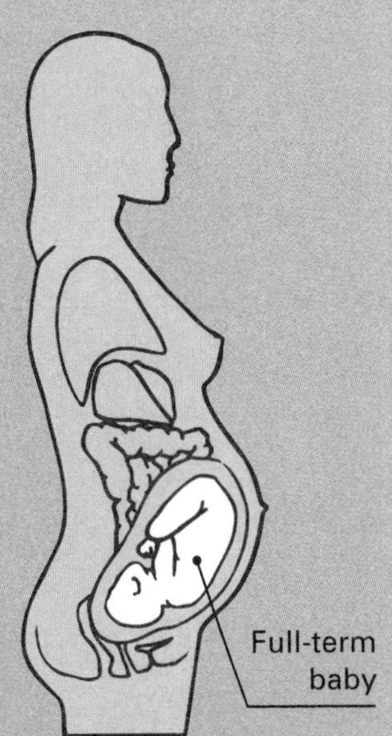

© DIAGRAM

Fertilization

Fertilization (or conception) occurs when the nucleus (control center containing the genetic material) of a sperm (the male sex cell) penetrates the cell body of an ovum (the female sex cell, also called an egg). The genetic material of both sex cells are combined to make a single cell with a full and unique set of genes. The resulting fertilized cell is called a zygote. The fertilization process involves several steps.

1 The sperm releases an enzyme (a specific protein that acts as a biological catalyst) from its acrosome, a vesicle on its head. This enzyme helps the sperm to burrow through the cells surrounding the egg.

2 The acrosome disintegrates and the head binds itself to the egg's outer zone.

3 The sperm tunnels through the outer zone.

4 The sperm fuses with the egg.

5 The nucleus of the sperm enters the egg and the sperm tail drops off. The surface of the egg changes to shut out other sperm.

Stages of fertilization

Sperm
Cells
Acrosome
Sperm tail
1
2
3
4
5
Outer zone
Egg
Sperm nucleus

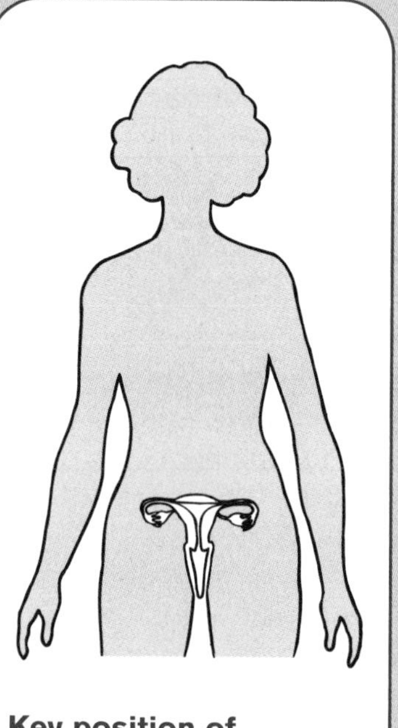

Key position of reproductive organs

Fertilization generally takes place in the fallopian tubes.

The egg's journey

1 Within an ovary, a follicle (saclike structure) ruptures, releasing an egg. Ovulation has occurred.

2 The egg passes into the fallopian tube. There is no direct link between the ovary and its fallopian tube. In the seconds after ovulation, the egg is moving freely in the body cavity.

3 In the tube, the egg is fertilized by a sperm swimming the other way.

4 The resulting zygote starts to divide by mitosis as it passes down the fallopian tube toward the uterus.

5 In the uterus, the ball of cells resulting from the original zygote becomes embedded in the endometrium (uterine lining), and the placenta develops.

From ovary to uterus

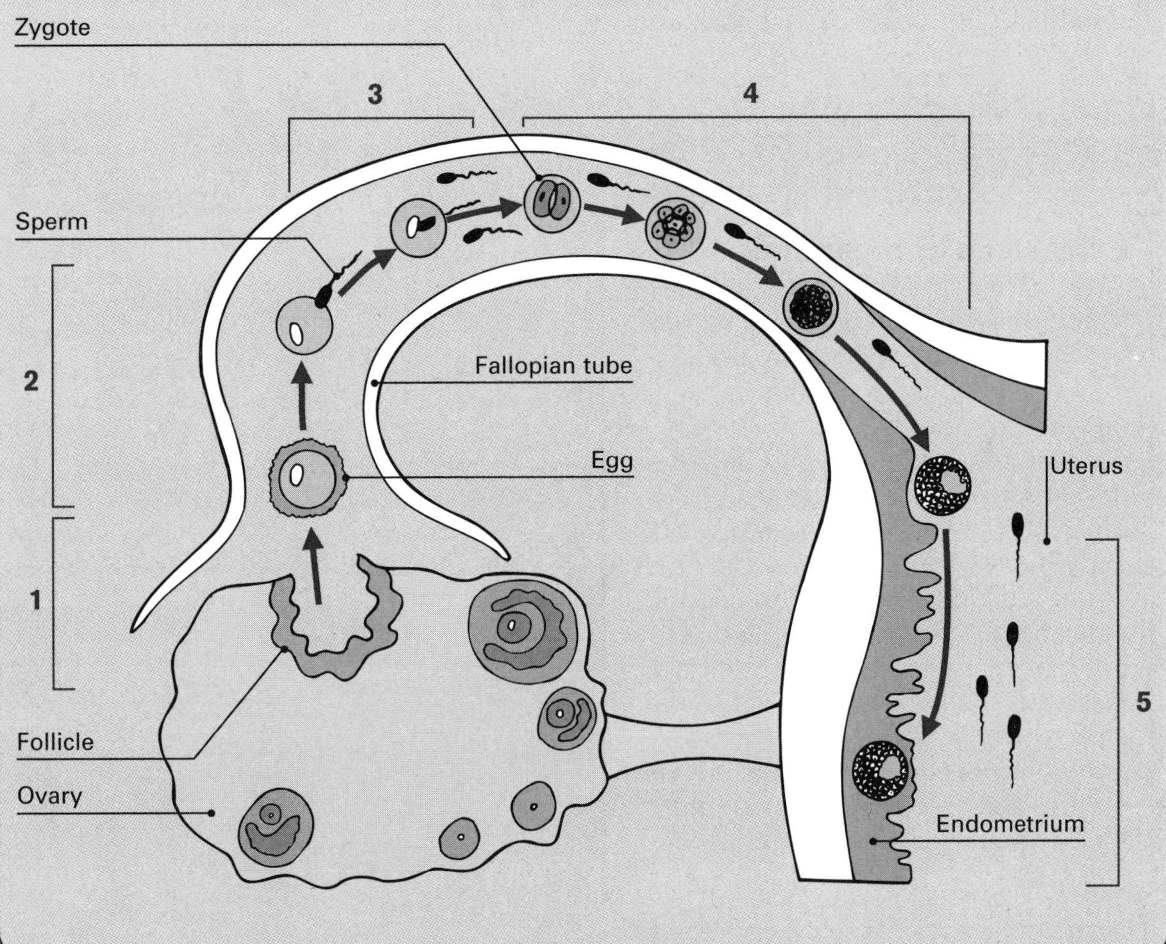

© DIAGRAM

Development of the fertilized egg

Development of the egg

As soon as fertilization occurs, the nucleus of the sperm fuses with that of the egg. This effectively creates a new cell, which is called a zygote. The zygote immediately begins to divide.

1 First, it is divided by mitosis into two cells. Mitosis is the most common type of cell division. It produces two daughter cells from the original. Each cell has a full set of genes. In the case of humans this is 46 chromosomes. Mitosis continues, with the two daughter cells dividing into four cells, then eight, and so on, forming a ball of cells.

1

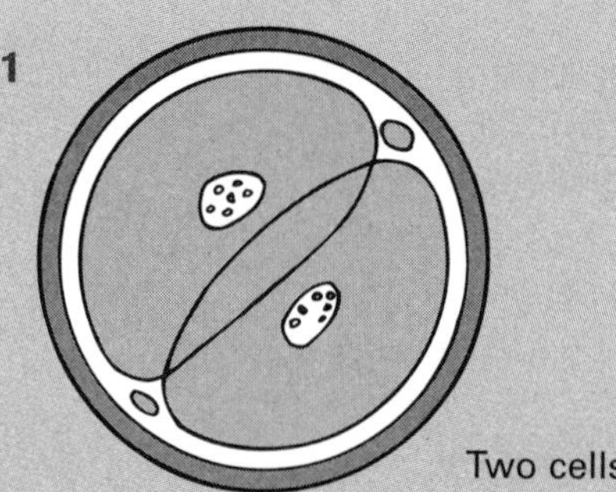

Two cells

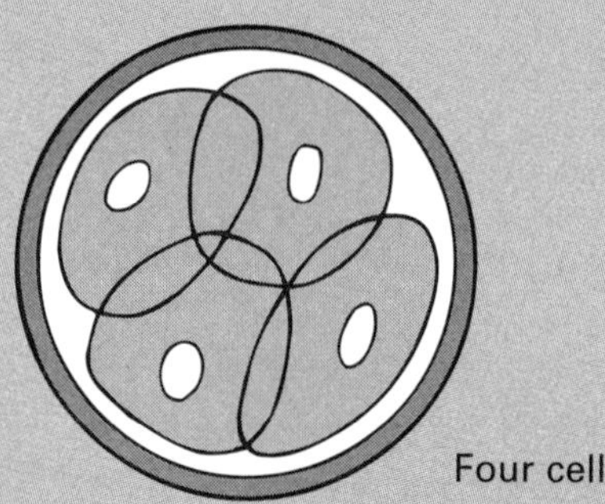

Four cells

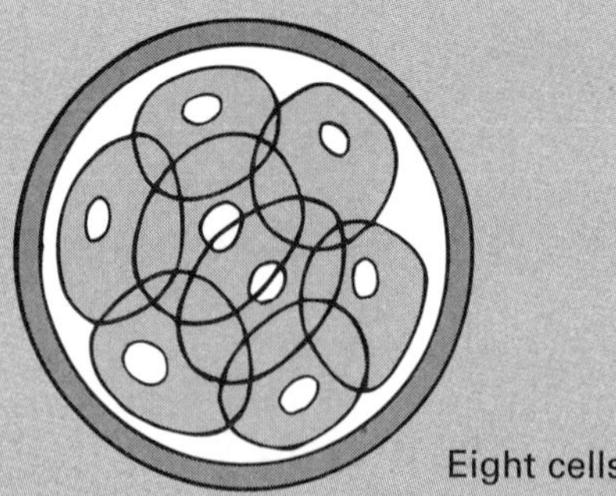

Eight cells

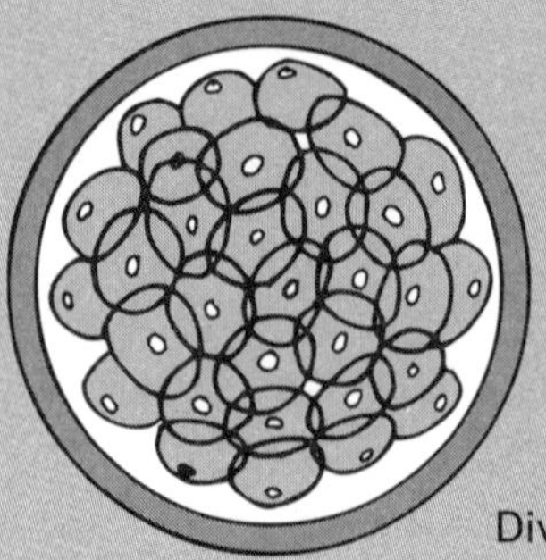

Division continues

Early signs of pregnancy

The sign most usually noticed first by a woman who has conceived is that her next period fails to arrive. She may notice a tingling, fullness, or heaviness in her breasts or abdomen, or she may need to pass urine more often than usual. Morning sickness may appear very early in pregnancy, and she may notice a sudden distaste for alcohol, smoking, or certain foods. The pregnancy is usually confirmed by a urine test, using a home kit or arranged by a doctor. As soon as a pregnancy is certain, medical advice on prenatal care should be sought for the welfare of both mother and baby.

2 After three days, a ball of cells (called a morula) has formed from the single zygote. This travels along the fallopian tube into the uterus.

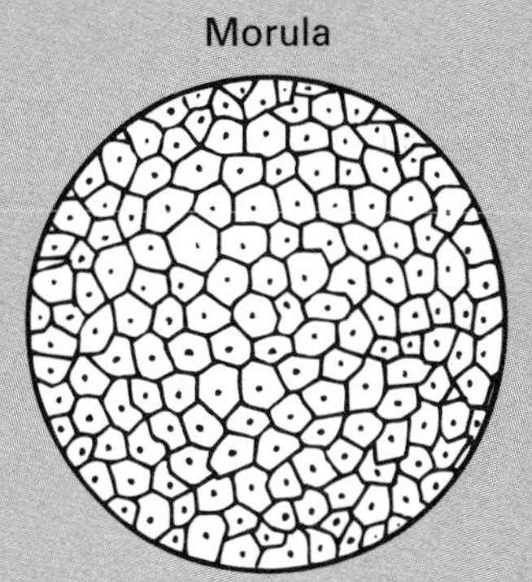

3 After four to five days, the morula turns into a hollow ball called a blastocyst. It has outer cells that form a wall called a trophoblast within which are a fluid-filled yolk sac and a cluster of inner cells. Certain cells in this cluster will develop into the embryo. Others will form part of the placenta.

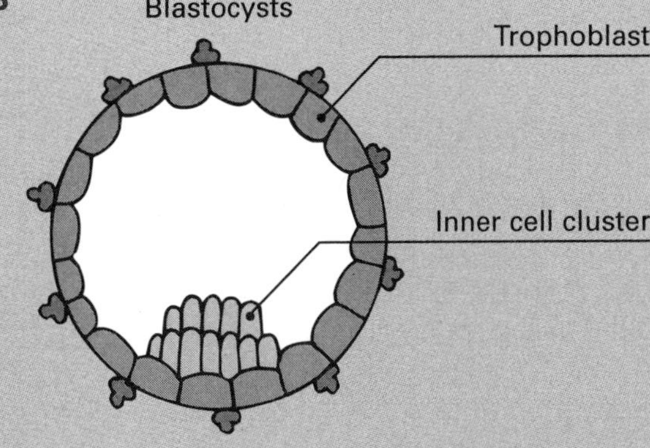

4 The blastocyst sinks into the uterine lining, where the inner cells are nourished by a rich supply of blood vessels. The placenta, a nourishing organ, grows from both uterus cells and those in the blastocyst.

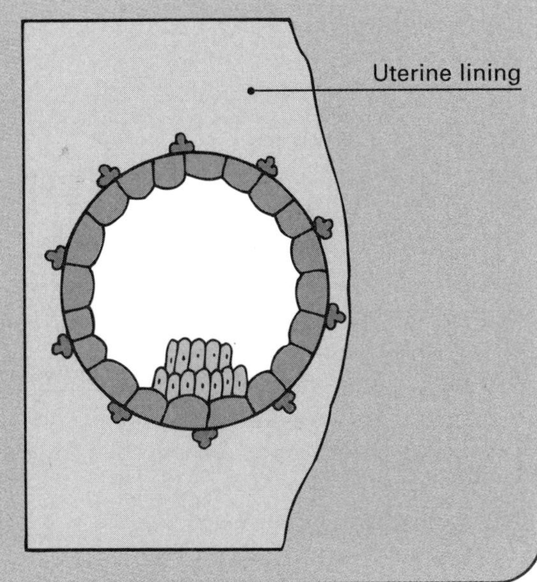

© DIAGRAM

Early embryo

Development of the embryo

Blastocyst implantation

The outer layer of the blastocyst is called the trophoblast. A thick point in the trophoblast forms the inner cell mass, also called the embryoblast. The embryo will develop from this mass. Some outer trophoblast cells penetrate the endometrium.

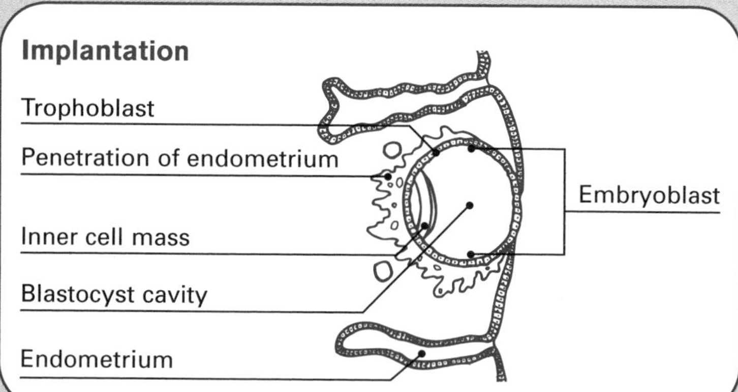

Early development

The trophoblast forms an outer membrane called the chorion. Two cavities form in the inner cell mass. The yolk sac surrounds the more central cavity, while the amnion surrounds the other. In humans, the yolk sac remains small. The amnion grows to surround the embryo as it develops.

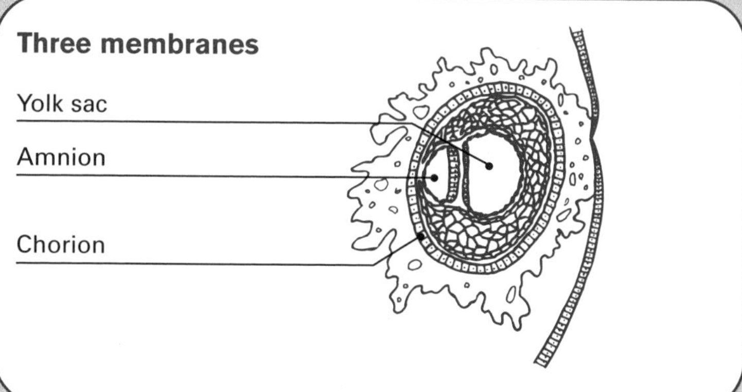

Embryo and placenta

A connecting stalk develops from the cells beside the two inner cavities. This is the start of the umbilical cord. The embryo develops from the cells between these two cavities. These cells first differentiate into two layers: the endoderm and ectoderm.

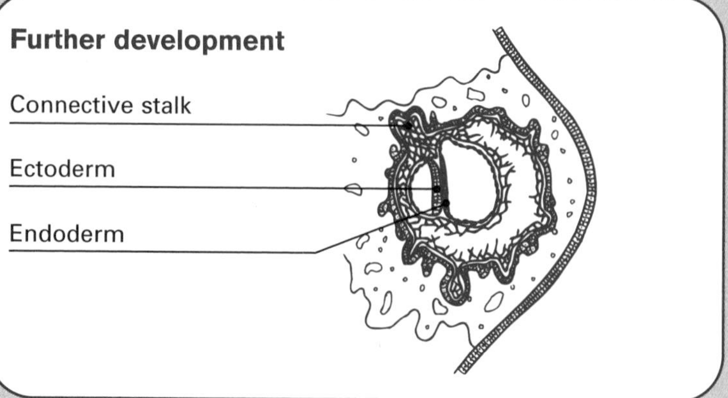

Pregnancy guidance

Do

- See a doctor as soon as you suspect you may be pregnant.
- Follow any health care advice given by your doctor or clinic.
- Attend all your recommended prenatal visits and classes.
- Take a bland drink during the night or first thing in the morning if you suffer from morning sickness.
- Take extra care of your teeth and gums during pregnancy.
- Try to rest with your feet up at least once a day.
- Eat a diet rich in calcium and vitamins.
- Eat plenty of fruit and cereal to avoid constipation.
- Take regular gentle exercise in the fresh air.
- Wear comfortable, loose-fitting clothes.
- Wear shoes with low, wide heels.
- Wear a well-fitting brassiere.
- Wash and massage your nipples daily.
- Wear support stockings if you suffer from tired legs.
- See a doctor immediately if you develop any of the warning signs listed on page 61, or have any other cause for alarm.
- Completely avoid alcohol and smoking.

Don't

- Use a vaginal douche.
- Use any drugs, including over-the-counter preparations and home remedies, without consulting a doctor.
- Use powerful laxatives to relieve constipation.
- "Eat for two."
- Put on more weight than recommended by your doctor.
- Eat a diet high in carbohydrates.
- Eat spiced or fatty foods if you suffer from morning sickness.
- Eat spiced foods or carbonated drinks if you suffer from indigestion, gas, or heartburn.
- Have intercourse in the last few weeks of pregnancy.
- Have intercourse earlier in pregnancy if your doctor advises against it.
- Continue sports that include a high risk of falling, such as horseback riding, skiing, or rock climbing.
- Travel in airplanes late in pregnancy. Lower cabin pressure can prevent oxygen from reaching the baby.
- Wear shoes with high, spindly heels.
- Wear tight-fitting clothes that may restrict the circulation.

Amniotic fluid

- The fetus drinks amniotic fluid during its development. It is absorbed into its bloodstream and passes through the placenta into the mother's blood.

Amniocentesis

- Doctors take a sample of the amniotic fluid using a syringe to find out about the health of a fetus. The fluid contains the DNA of the fetus, which can show congenital problems.

© DIAGRAM

Late embryo

Embryo: 3 weeks

At three weeks the embryo is differentiated from the rest of the blastocyst. Now the growing blastocyst protrudes from the endometrium. Nutrients pass through the chorion to nourish the embryo. The amniotic cavity begins to engulf it, while the yolk sac begins to shrink. The connective stalk lengthens as the umbilical cord begins to develop.

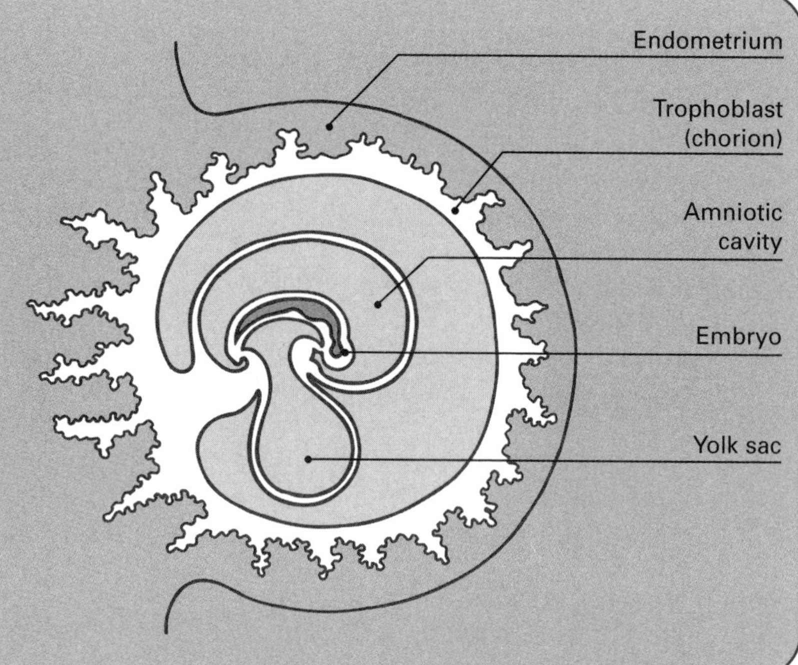

Embryo: 4 weeks

In the fourth week the head, heart, and coiled tail section of the embryo become visible. The yolk sac continues to shrink. The chorion below the lengthening connective stalk enlarges and extends into the endometrium forming the first part of the placenta. The placenta will supply oxygen and nutrients to the embryo and take its waste away.

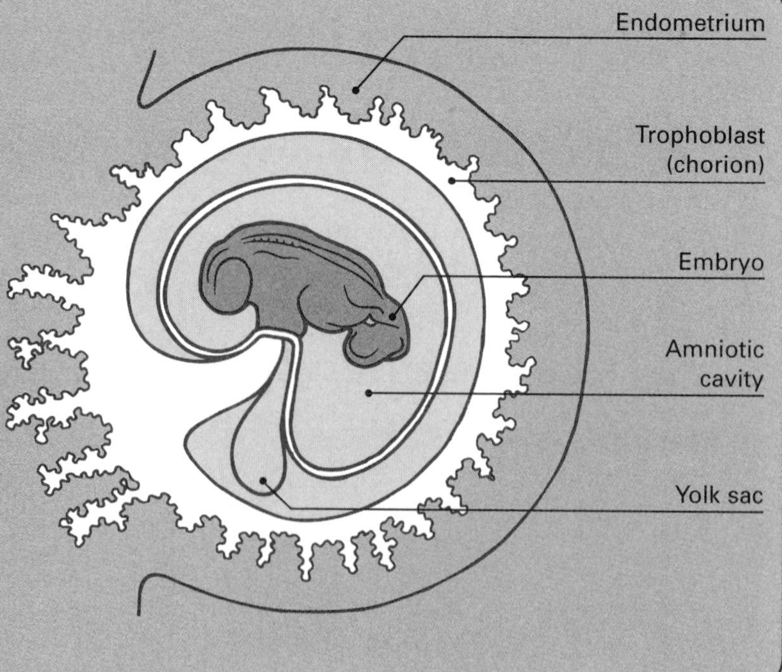

Embryo growth: 4 to 8 weeks

Embryo at 4 weeks

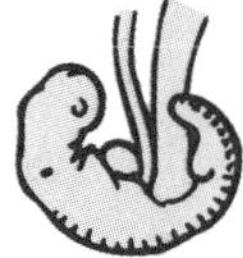

Embryo at 5 weeks

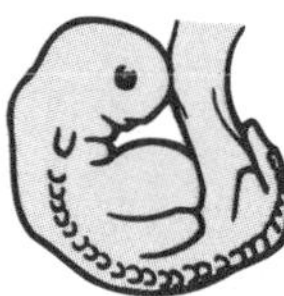

Embryo at 6 weeks

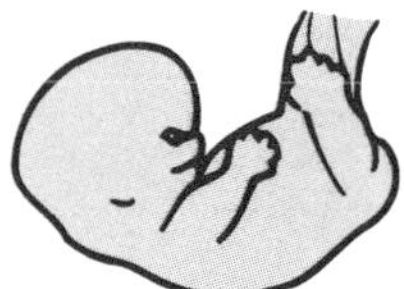

Embryo at 7 weeks

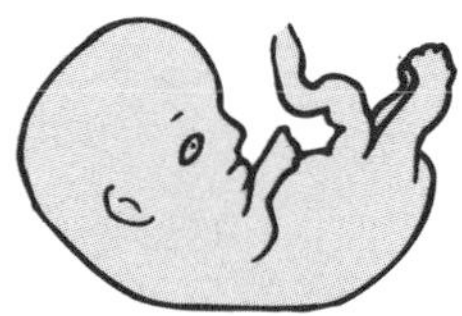

Embryo at 8 weeks

Pregnancy development

At four weeks the uterus has not yet begun to enlarge. By eight weeks, the developing early fetus begins to fill the uterus cavity and causes the uterus to grow. This has the effect of squeezing the bladder against the pubic bone, causing more frequent urination. The larger uterus pushes up against the mother's intestines and diaphragm. This raises the stomach and causes acidic stomach juices to rise up the esophagus, resulting in indigestion.

Pregnancy at four weeks

Pregnancy at eight weeks

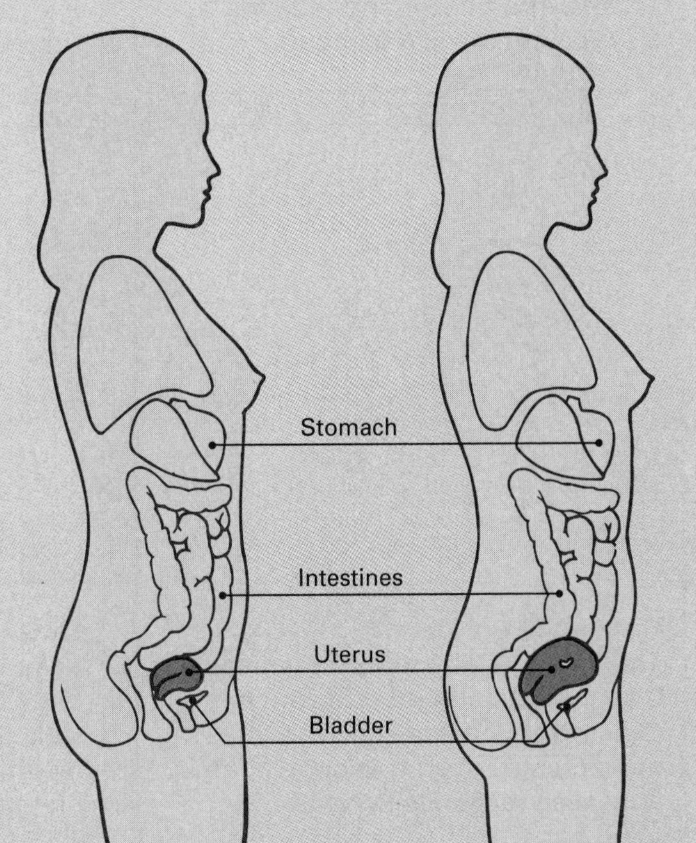

© DIAGRAM

Development from 12 to 24 weeks

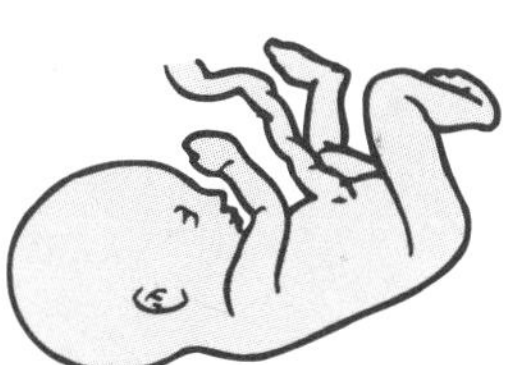

Fetus at 12 weeks
At this time the fetus's genitals are visible by ultrasound. The eyes are formed as are most of the internal organs. The fingers and toes are forming but are still webbed.

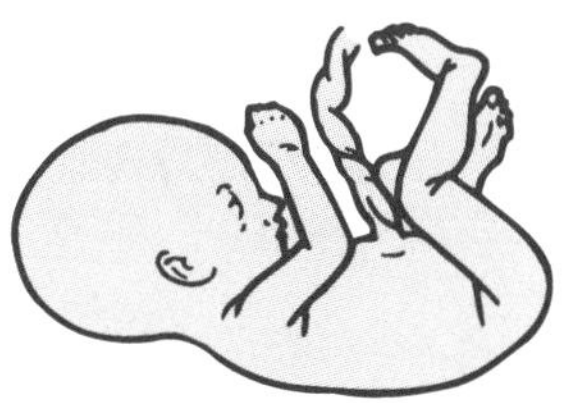

Fetus at 16 weeks
All the organs and body systems of the fetus are defined. From now on the body will just grow in size. The ears begin to work and the fetus's fingerprints form.

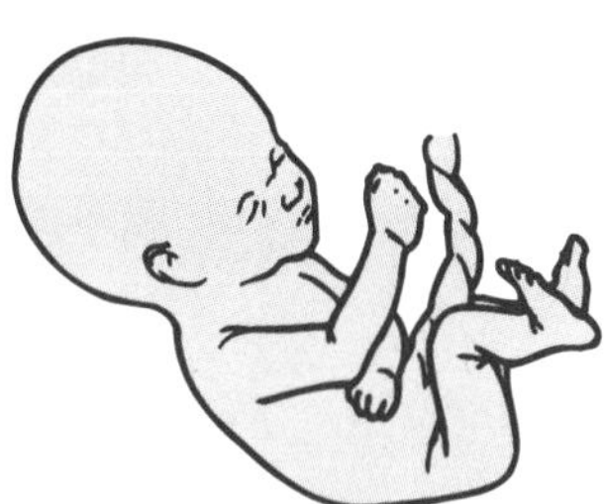

Fetus at 20 weeks
The fetus's teeth are forming inside the jawbone, and muscles are being laid down. Consequently the fetus's movements become stronger. The fetus also responds to touch.

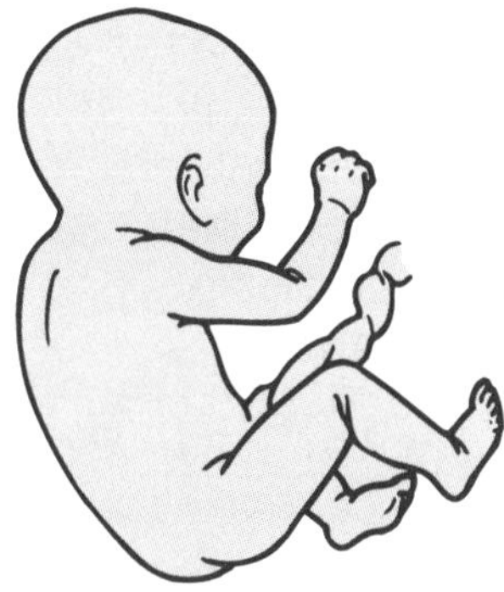

Fetus at 24 weeks
Palm lines appear on the hands. The fetus follows a pattern of sleep and wakefulness. It can even hiccup. The diaphragm begins to produce breathing motions.

Development from 12 to 24 weeks

During this period the woman becomes visibly pregnant with the uterus swelling in size. Her hormones start to stabilize ending the large fluctuations of the early pregnancy. Because of this, mood swings and feelings of nausea that may have accompanied the first few months of pregnancy are now on the wane. The skin may darken and the enlarged fetus can be felt above the pubic bone. The mother can feel the movements of the fetus, which may begin to knock against her ribs.

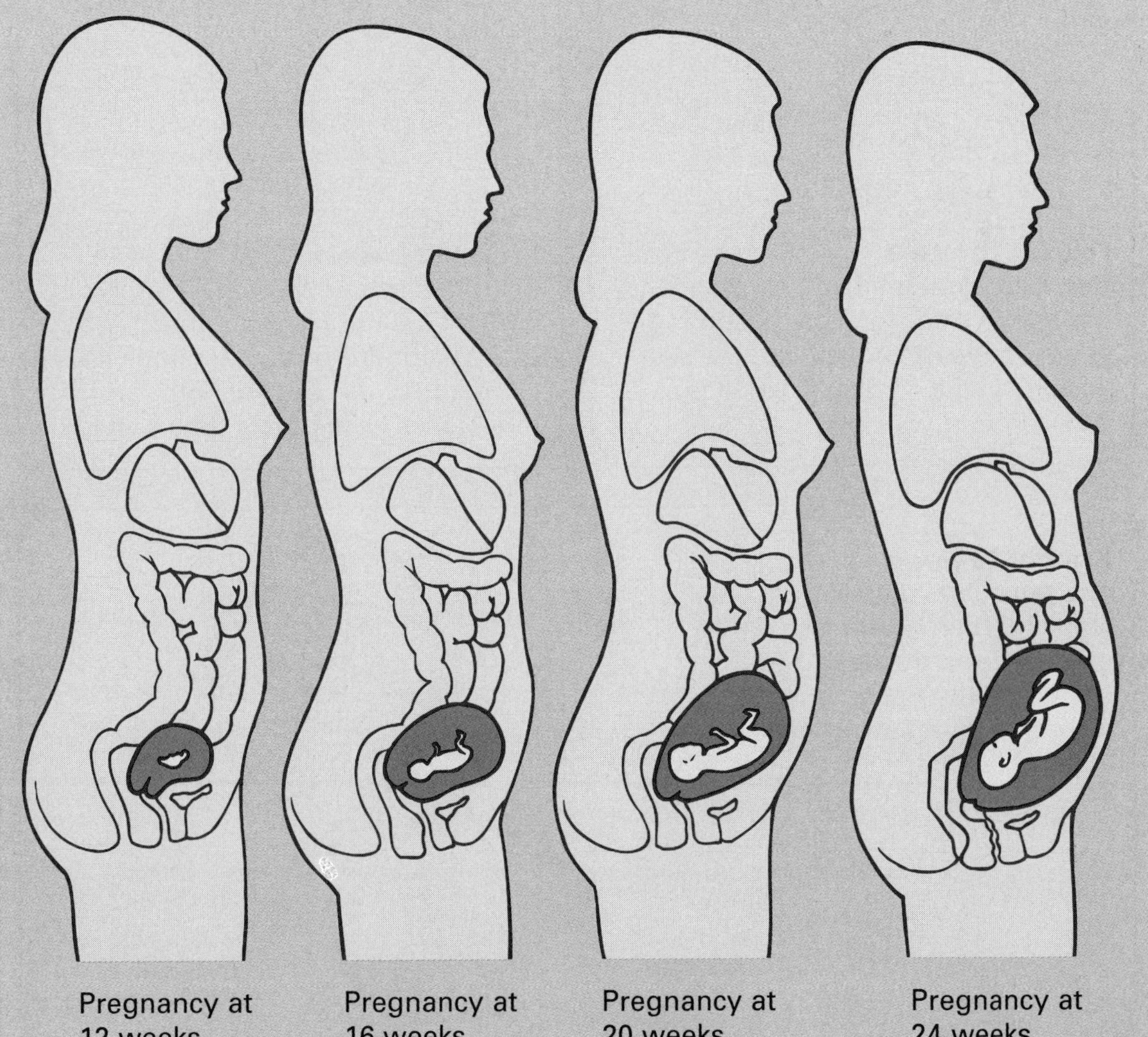

Pregnancy at 12 weeks

Pregnancy at 16 weeks

Pregnancy at 20 weeks

Pregnancy at 24 weeks

© DIAGRAM

Mid-term fetus

Development from 28 to 36 weeks

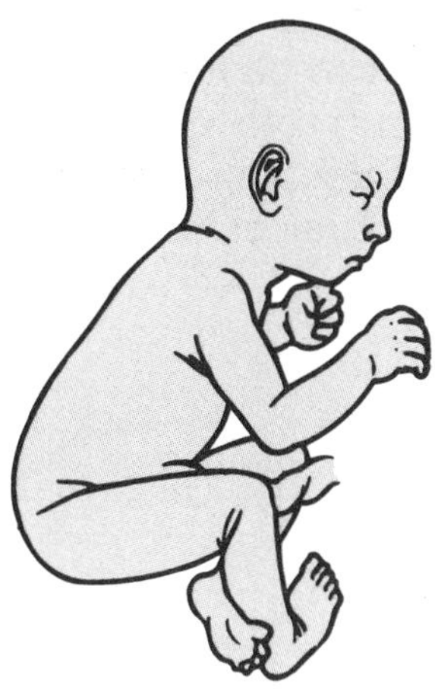

Fetus at 28 weeks
Deposits of fat are laid down under the baby's skin. To avoid becoming soggy in the amniotic fluid, the skin is coated with a waxy substance called vernix.

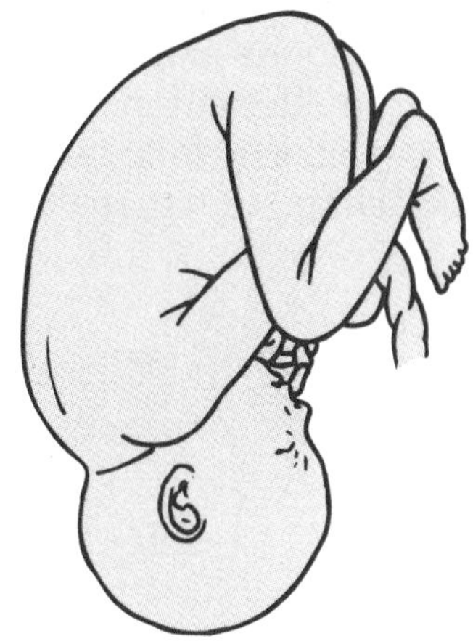

Fetus at 32 weeks
The fetus can now see. Generally at this time it turns head down in preparation for birth. The lungs are almost fully developed. Four out of five babies born at this time survive.

Fetus at 36 weeks
The fetus puts on weight steadily. There is at least some hair on the head and body, and the fingernails have grown to cover the ends of fingers.

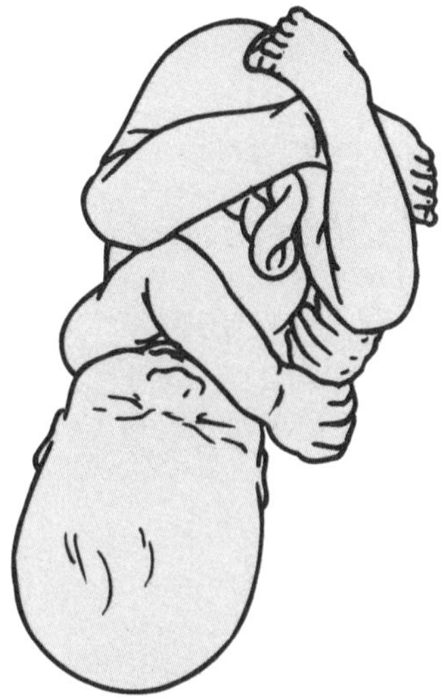

Development from 28 to 36 weeks

The woman becomes noticeably bigger in this period. She may notice stretch marks on her stomach and thighs, and have a sore back. This is caused by the loosening of the pelvis in preparation for birth. The lower ribcage feels sore and the navel becomes flat. A dark line may appear between the navel and pubic hair. In the eighth month of pregnancy the baby drops and breathlessness and indigestion problems reduce. The large abdomen may make it harder for the woman to find a comfortable position to sleep in.

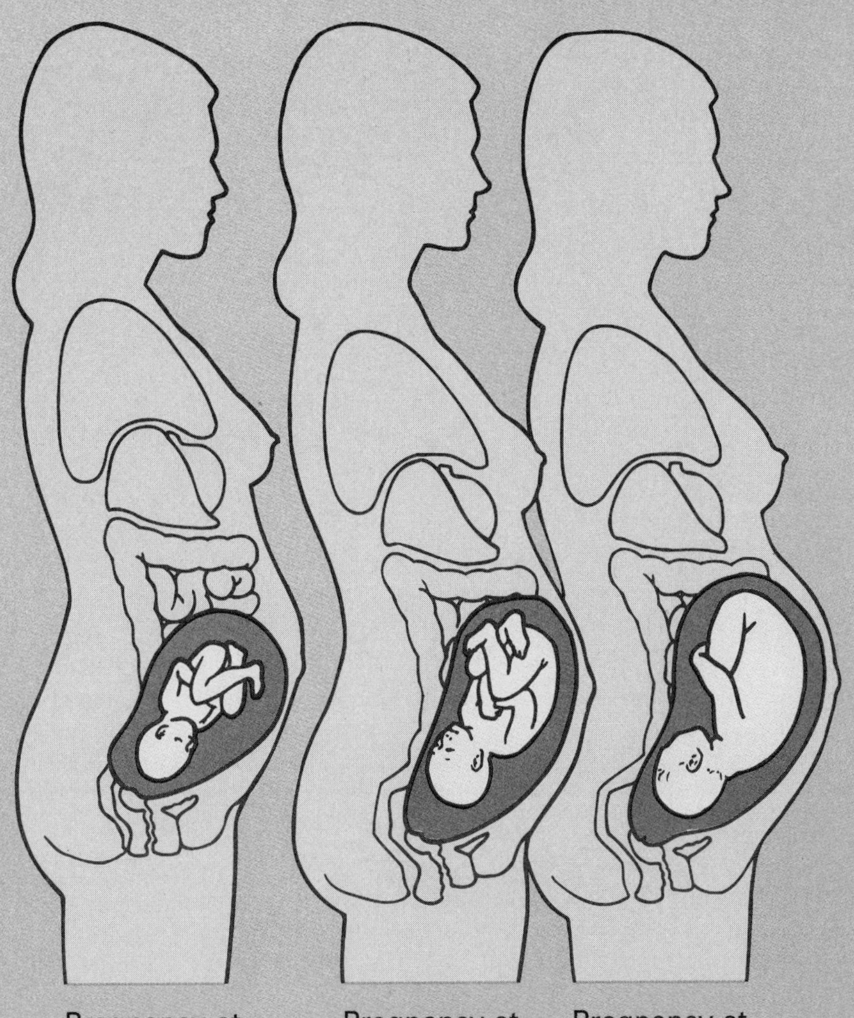

Pregnancy at 28 weeks

Pregnancy at 32 weeks

Pregnancy at 36 weeks

© DIAGRAM

Placenta

The placenta is a temporary organ formed from tissues that have developed from both the mother's body and cells in the blastocyst. It is connected to the fetus by the umbilical cord, and it brings the blood of the fetus into close proximity with the mother's. Oxygen and nutrients pass from the mother's blood into the fetus's, while waste products move the other way.

Section through uterus and membranes to show full-term fetus and placenta

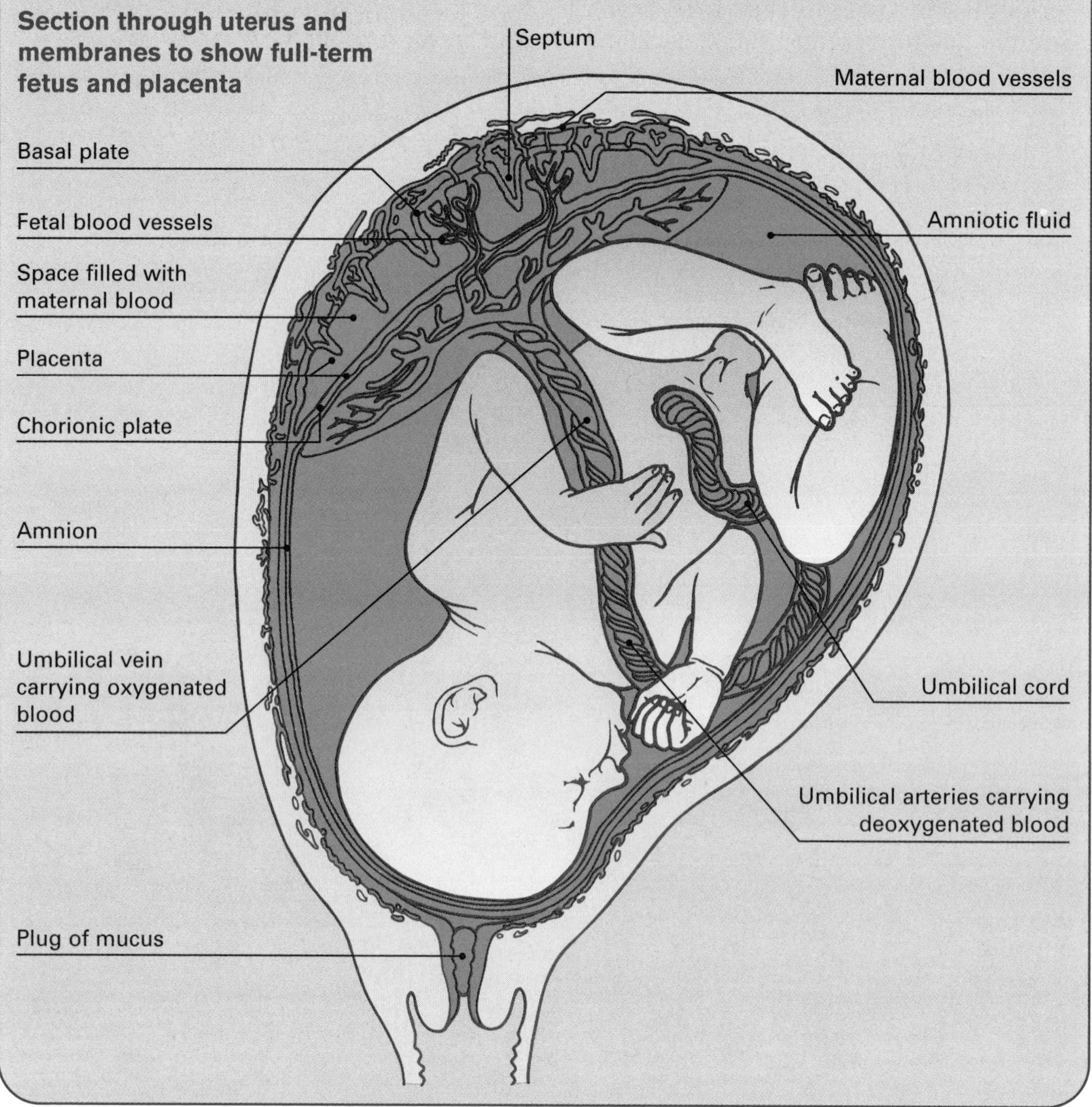

Fetal circulation

The fetus's blood not only pumps around the body, but it also circulates through the placenta via vessels in the umbilical cord. Arteries carry blood away from the heart while veins bring it back again. Generally arteries carry oxygenated blood. However, the umbilical arteries carry deoxygenated blood away from the heart to the placenta. This blood is oxygenated by the mother's, and the large umbilical vein carries it back into the fetus where it travels through the liver and connects to the vena cava just under the heart. The pulmonary vessels bypass the fetus's developing lungs.

Fetal circulation before birth

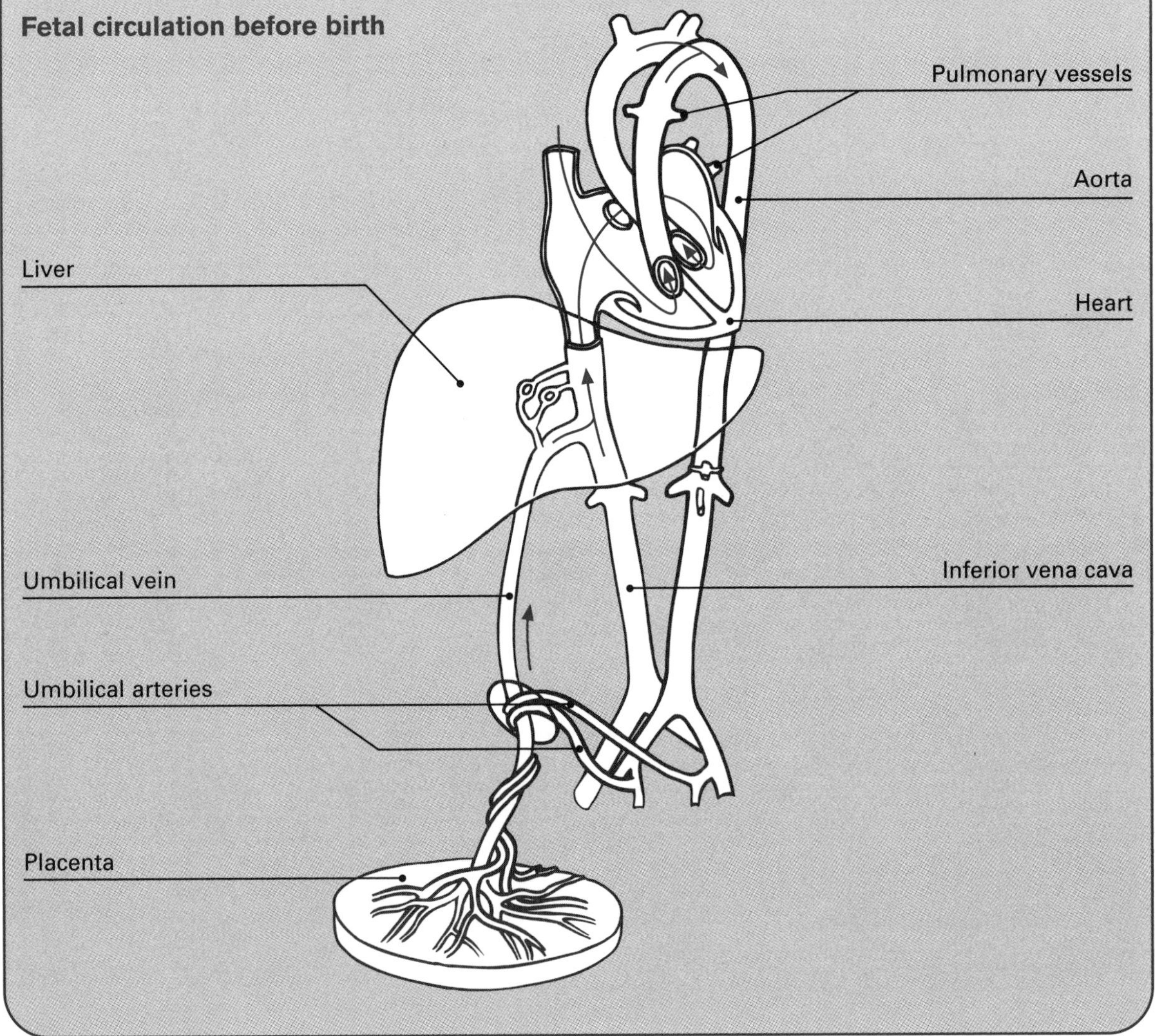

© DIAGRAM

Fully grown fetus

By the 40th week the fetus is fully grown. It is held tightly in the uterus, which restricts its movements. The placenta is squeezed between the fetus and the uterus wall. If this is a woman's first baby, the fetus's head will be engaged in the pelvis, pushing down on the cervix. Later babies may not engage until just before they begin to be pushed out by labor contractions.

Section through the mother's abdomen, showing a baby ready to be born

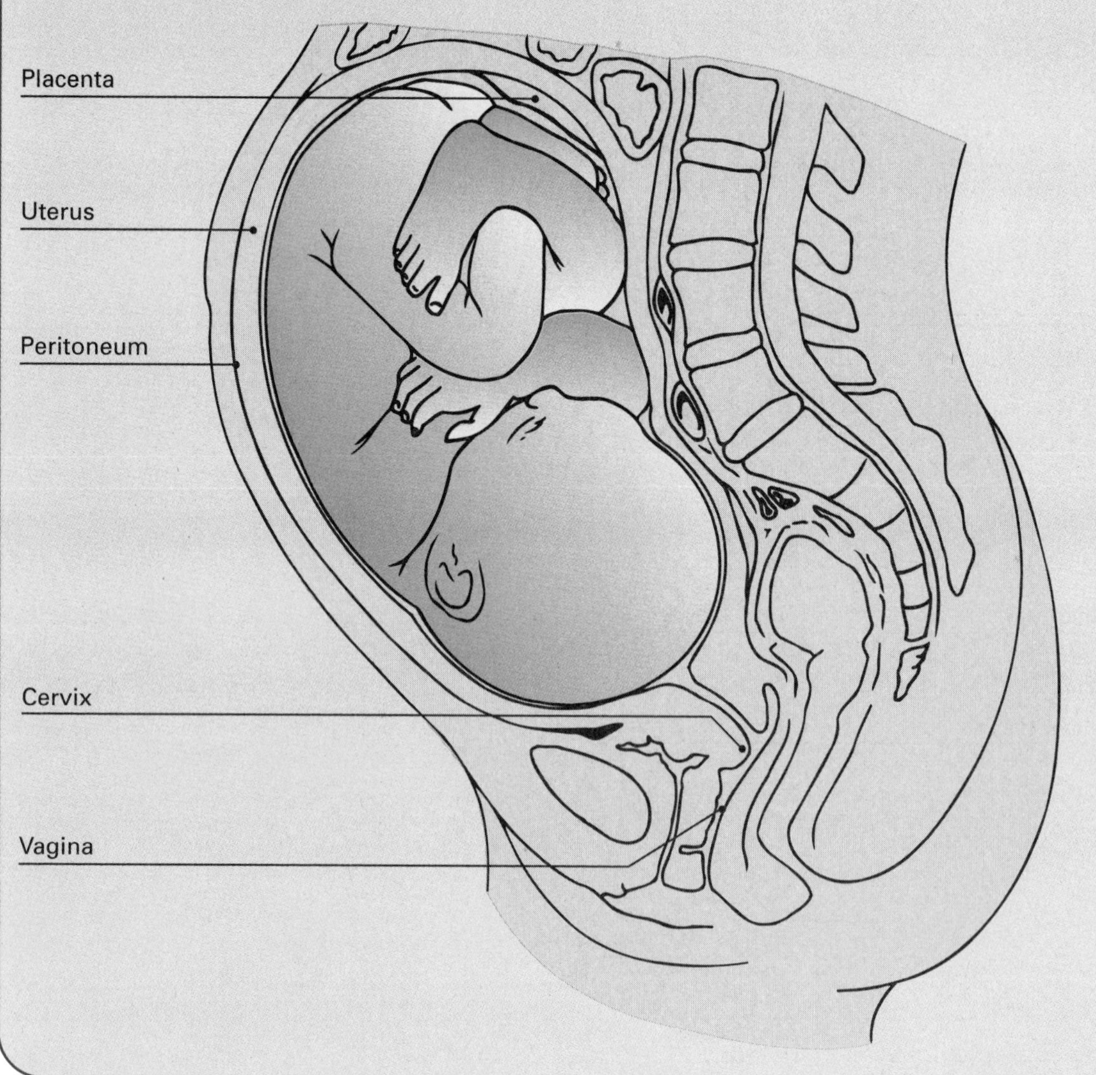

Preparing for labor

The mother may experience Braxton-Hicks contractions in the last few weeks of pregnancy. These are less severe and not as regular as true labor contractions. As labor approaches the muscles of the cervix begin to soften and the pelvis widens to make room for the baby's head. The fetus presses down on the pelvis so much that it may disrupt blood supply to the legs slightly, causing pins and needles.

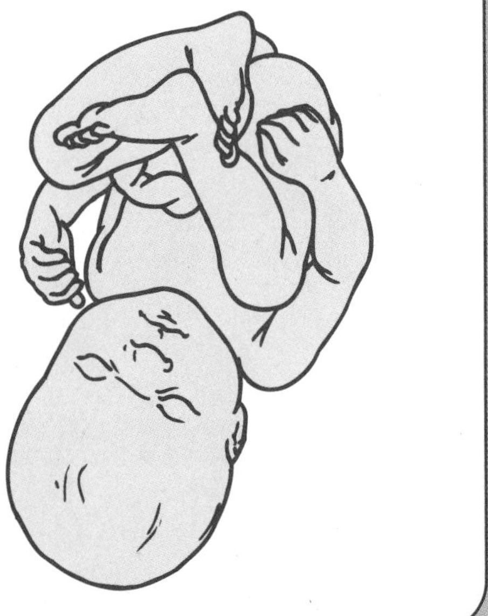
Full-term fetus

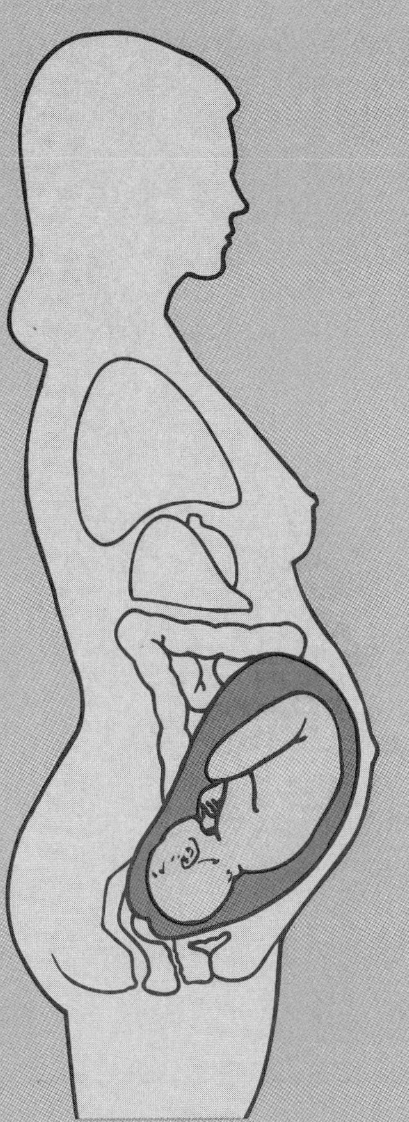

A show

- As the cervix softens and opens, the plug of mucus inside it may leak out. This bloodied mucus is called a "show" and is often the first sign that labor is beginning.

Nesting

- In the weeks before birth, many expectant mothers want to clean their home and make things ready for the arrival of the new baby.

© DIAGRAM

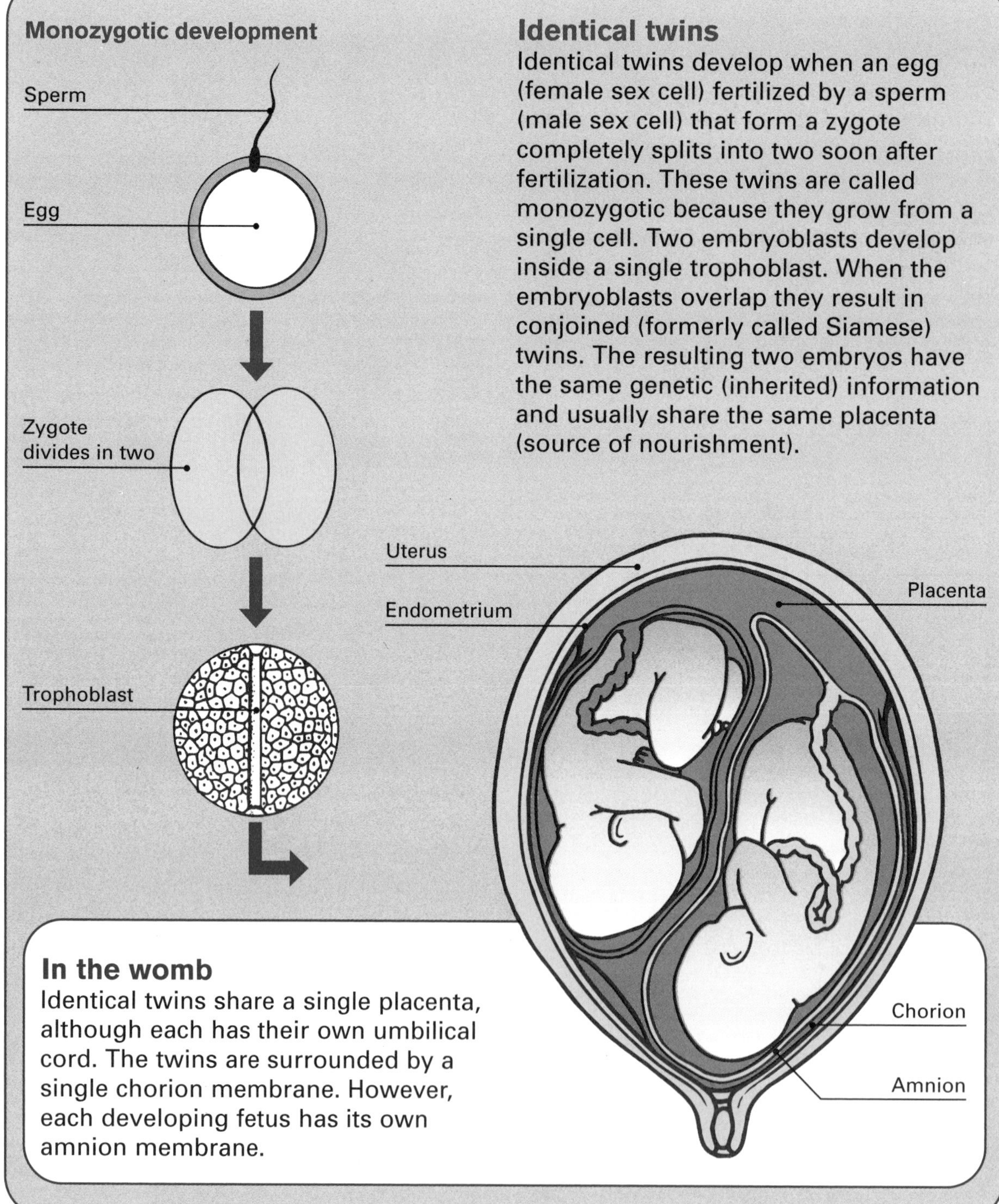

Identical twins

Identical twins develop when an egg (female sex cell) fertilized by a sperm (male sex cell) that form a zygote completely splits into two soon after fertilization. These twins are called monozygotic because they grow from a single cell. Two embryoblasts develop inside a single trophoblast. When the embryoblasts overlap they result in conjoined (formerly called Siamese) twins. The resulting two embryos have the same genetic (inherited) information and usually share the same placenta (source of nourishment).

In the womb

Identical twins share a single placenta, although each has their own umbilical cord. The twins are surrounded by a single chorion membrane. However, each developing fetus has its own amnion membrane.

Nonidentical twins

Nonidentical (or dizygotic—"two zygotes") twins develop when two eggs are fertilized by two different sperm. Therefore the twins each have a different set of genetic information. Although they are born at the same time, nonidentical twins are no more closely related to each other than normal siblings. Each egg divides as normal to produce a separate blastocyst containing a single embryo. Each embryo has its own placenta.

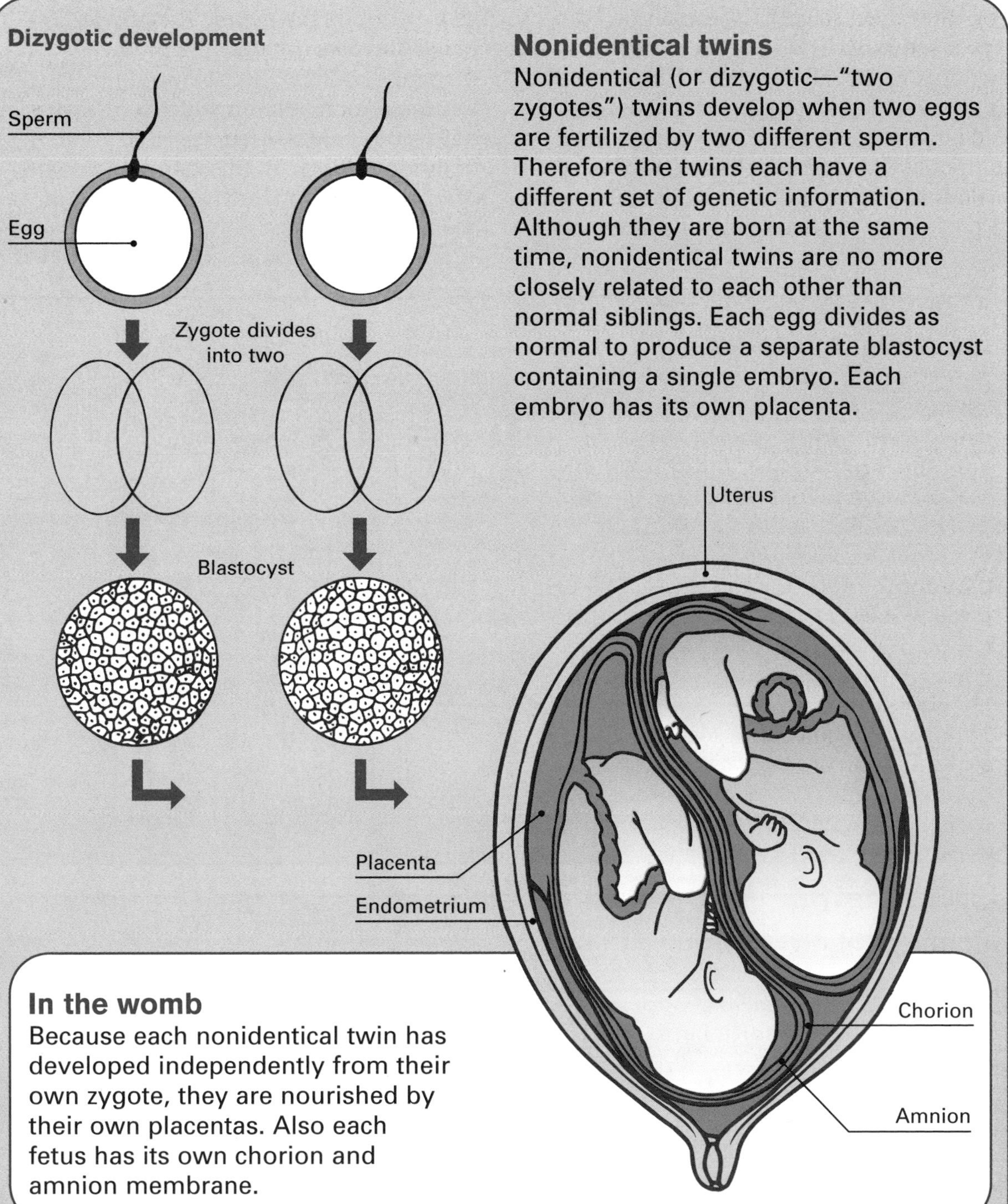

In the womb

Because each nonidentical twin has developed independently from their own zygote, they are nourished by their own placentas. Also each fetus has its own chorion and amnion membrane.

© DIAGRAM

Changes in pregnancy

The three main stages of a woman's reproductive life—puberty, pregnancy, and menopause—are all associated with changes in hormone levels, physical characteristics, and behavior patterns. In pregnancy the hormonal changes cause the menstrual periods to stop, and they reprogram the body to provide for the development and growth of the baby inside the uterus. The physical changes involve not only the mother's enlarging abdomen, but also modifications elsewhere. Some ways in which a pregnant woman can help to keep herself in good condition through all the changes associated with pregnancy and birth are discussed in the following pages.

Age and pregnancy

The age of the mother may affect several factors in a pregnancy and birth, especially in a first pregnancy.

a Mothers under age 20 run a higher risk of anemia, toxemia of pregnancy, and congenital abnormality of the baby, but labor is usually easier.

b Mothers aged 20 to 30 have the lowest rates of stillbirth and early infant death.

c Mothers aged 30 to 40 have longer labors, a greater chance of twins, heavier babies, and more complications of pregnancy and birth.

d Mothers over 40 have a high risk of Down syndrome babies and other complications, but have shorter labors.

Changes in pregnancy

The diagram on the right plots the sites of many of the physical changes and minor physical problems that may be encountered during a pregnancy.

1 Fainting.

2 Brittle hair.

3 Nasal congestion and nosebleeds, resulting from a rise in blood supply.

4 Increase in skin pigmentation, especially in dark-haired women.

5 Aggravation of dry or greasy skin problems.

6 Slight rise in basal body temperature.

7 Bleeding from swollen and tender gums.

8 Heartburn.

9 Shortness of breath.

10 Increase in size and weight of the breasts, and possible tenderness.
11 Raised blood pressure.
12 Changes in appetite. These may take the form of cravings, distaste for certain foods, or an increase or decrease in the amounts eaten.

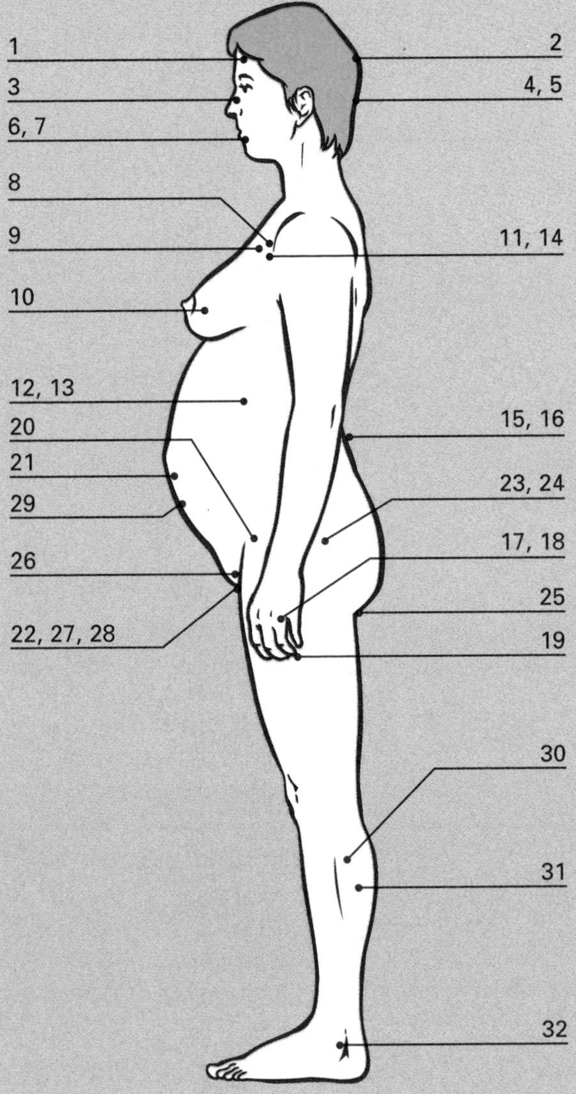

13 Nausea and vomiting, especially in the morning during the early months of pregnancy.
14 Palpitations.
15 Postural changes as the body adapts to the extra load of pregnancy.
16 Backache caused by changes in the muscles and tendons of the back.
17 Clumsiness, caused by changes in the nerves and circulation and also by increased size and weight.
18 Tingling hands.
19 Brittle nails.
20 Congestion of the pelvis and abdomen caused by the increased blood supply.
21 Stretch marks: small red lines that develop over the abdomen during pregnancy and later fade to silvery marks.
22 Cessation of the menstrual periods.
23 Constipation.
24 Gas in the intestines.
25 Hemorrhoids.
26 Frequent urination, a result of the enlarging uterus pressing on the bladder.
27 Vaginal discharge.
28 Darkening in color of the vagina, from pale pink to dark pink or violet.
29 Weight gain caused by the baby itself; the fluid around it in the uterus; fluid retained in the mother's tissues; the placenta; the increase in volume of the mother's blood; and some laying down of fat.
30 Cramps in the calves.
31 Varicose veins.
32 Swelling of the ankles and feet.

© DIAGRAM

Prenatal care

Prenatal facilities are designed to provide the best possible care for the pregnant mother and her baby. They provide frequent checks on the well-being of mother and baby, give advice on daily care and routines, and watch for any signs of conditions that may endanger the baby or complicate the birth. A detailed history of the present and previous pregnancies is taken, and close attention is paid to all of the following points:

1 Height. This is measured at the first prenatal visit. Body measurements provide clues as to whether the mother's physique will allow an easy birth.

2 Relaxation. The ability to relax fully aids labor, and so is usually taught during the prenatal period.

3 Diet. A good diet throughout pregnancy ensures that mother and baby are well nourished.

4 Blood pressure. This is a good monitor of the mother's circulation, and is taken at every prenatal visit.

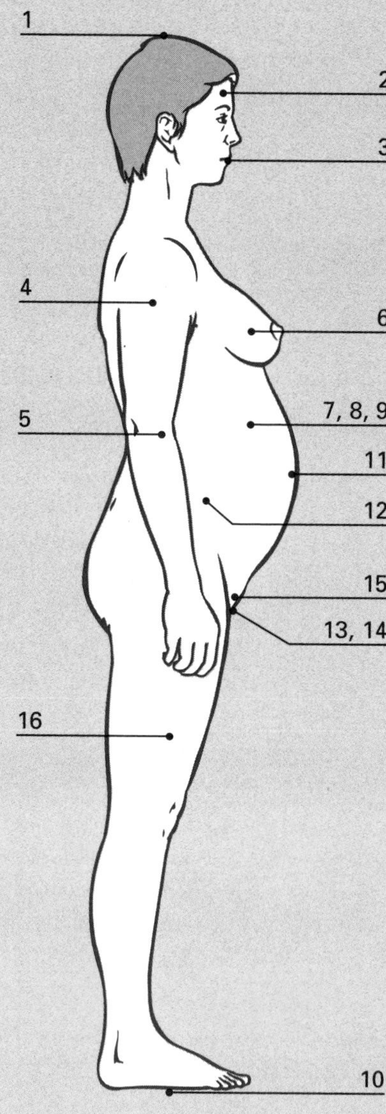

5 Blood tests. These will be used to check for infection, anemia etc.

6 Breast care. The mother will be advised on how to keep her breasts in good condition during pregnancy and prepare them for breastfeeding.

7 Amniocentesis. A sample of the fluid around the baby may be taken to check for abnormal signs if this is thought necessary (for instance during an older woman's pregnancy). Amniocentesis occasionally causes some risk to the fetus.

8 Ultrasound. This method of checking the progress of the baby is used in many clinics, and involves bouncing sound waves off the fetus.

9 X-ray. This technique was once used to check the size and position of the baby, but is now avoided as much as possible and used only when complications occur that cannot be checked in any other way.

10 Weight. The mother's weight is checked to ensure that it is not rising too rapidly or slowly.

11 Abdomen. An external examination of the abdomen is made at the first prenatal appointment.
12 Pelvic examination. This is done to establish the presence of the pregnancy and to check for abnormalities in the vagina or uterus.
13 Smear test. This is sometimes performed as an extra safety precaution.
14 Vaginal swab. The vaginal secretions are examined for any infection or abnormality.
15 Urine test. This is done regularly to test for diabetes or other irregularities.
16 Exercises. Prenatal advisors recommend suitable exercises for the pregnant mother.

Nausea and vomiting

Morning sickness affects many women in early pregnancy. Some may simply feel nauseous first thing in the morning, but others actually retch or vomit. Although this problem usually disappears by the third or fourth month, it is miserable while it lasts. But with a little care its effects can be minimized. Drinking a bland liquid such as milk or water during the night or immediately on waking will help to allay much of the nausea, and so will eating something bland such as dry toast, cookies, or an apple. Pregnant women prone to nausea should avoid all rich and fatty foods as much as possible.

Digestive problems

Digestive problems are rife in pregnancy. One of the chief causes is pressure from the uterus, which presses the diaphragm upward and so exerts pressure on the stomach. This can cause heartburn and indigestion. Eating bland foods and avoiding strong spices and heavy meals may ease the problem. Constipation is also a frequent problem during pregnancy. It is caused by the slowing down of the digestive system and the relaxation of the muscle walls. It can be alleviated by drinking plenty of fluids and eating sufficient fiber, but strong laxatives should never be used.

Miscarriage

Miscarriage, or natural abortion, is the death of an embryo or fetus in the uterus or its expulsion before it is capable of sustaining life. As many as 20 percent of pregnancies may end in miscarriage, but many of these are very early and may be mistaken for a slightly overdue period. Most miscarriages take place in the first three months of pregnancy, but later cases may occur if there is a weakness of the cervix, or if the mother has used violent bowel laxatives which initiate contractions. If a miscarriage is suspected, the mother should go straight to bed and a doctor must be called.

© DIAGRAM

Activity during pregnancy

Careful attention to posture, relaxation, and exercise will be invaluable to the expectant mother throughout her pregnancy and after the baby's birth. Muscles and tendons are prone to softening and sagging during pregnancy, and the mother's extra weight and increased size tend to aggravate the problem. Her posture alters as the pregnancy progresses, and she may experience aches and pains in her back and legs as a result. On these pages we look at some of the ways in which the expectant mother can use her body as efficiently as possible during pregnancy. These hints will help her to avoid strain and unnecessary health problems, and encourage the developing fetus to move into the best position for birth. Keeping fit will help new mothers recover their figures after birth.

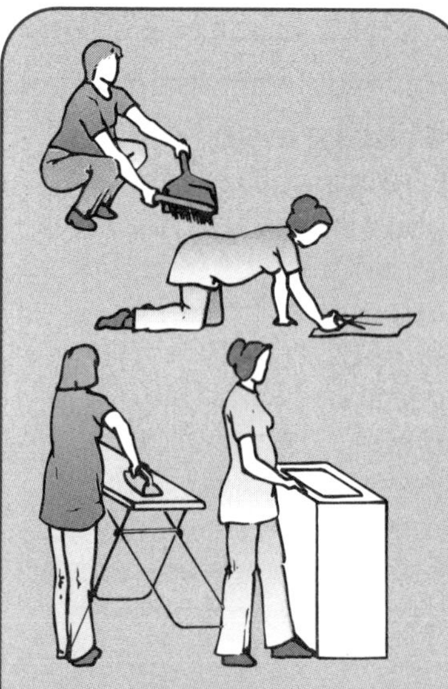

Daily activities

Because the back carries much of the burden of the extra weight during pregnancy, its muscles are susceptible to strain imposed by bending at the waist. The correct posture for various everyday activities are shown above. The back is kept as straight as possible and the strain is taken by the legs.

Lifting

Avoid lifting heavy objects as this can cause unnecessary strain on the back and abdomen. If lifting is unavoidable, try using the methods shown above. Squat right down with your knees apart and your spine straight and then straighten up slowly. Hold the load high in the arms.

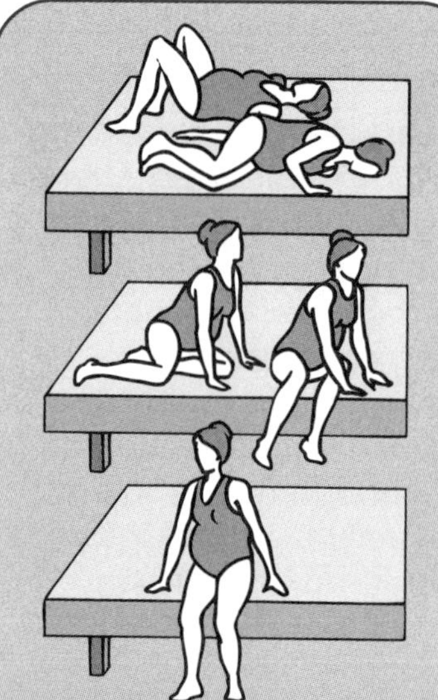

Getting out of bed

As the abdomen grows it becomes increasingly difficult to rise from a lying position. The method shown above is safe, and can also be modified for getting up from the floor. Bend your knees up and roll over onto one side; your arms can be used to raise your trunk from the bed. Then swing your legs onto the floor.

Posture

During pregnancy there is a great temptation to walk badly, with the pelvis tilted forward and the back hollowed (left). Wearing high-heeled shoes increases this tendency as they throw the trunk forward and leave the body off-balance. A hollowed back may be inevitable in the very late stages of pregnancy, when the abdomen is very large, but in the early and middle stages try to walk with the spine as straight as possible. The head should be erect, and the abdomen and chest supported by the trunk muscles (right). Wearing sensible shoes will help.

General exercises

These exercises will help to improve muscle tone and circulation. Kneel on all fours and arch the back to exercise the pelvic floor. Lie on your back with your knees bent and your feet flat on the ground. Slowly extend each leg. From the same position, tighten your buttocks and hold this position for a moment. Sit in a chair with your heels resting on the floor. Bend your feet upward and then point them down.

Relaxation

It is very valuable for pregnant women to spend some part of each day relaxing, especially in the later stages of pregnancy. Daily relaxation rests the mother's body, and also teaches her to relax; this ability will be very useful during the birth, when she needs to conserve energy between contractions. Raising the feet above the level of the head improves a sluggish circulation, and the mother should try to do this whenever she rests.

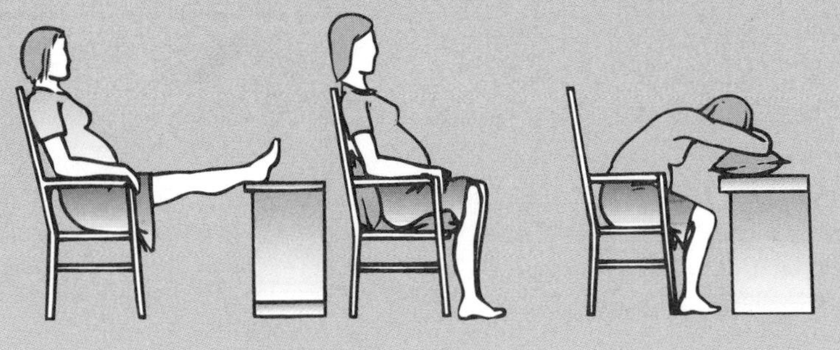

© DIAGRAM

Methods of birth control have been practiced for centuries, but the search still continues for the safest and most reliable form of contraception. In the United States about 80 percent of all couples use some kind of contraceptive. Many women prefer the reliability of the contraceptive pill or the intrauterine device (IUD), but their side-effects and possible health risks have persuaded some to return to using a diaphragm or other type of cap. The male forms of contraception, the condom and coitus interruptus, are still the most widely-practiced contraceptive methods. Male pills have been developed but have not become widely used. Hormone treatments, similar to the work of pills, may also be delivered by implants or patches stuck on the skin.

Contraceptive methods

Oral contraceptives or the birth control **pill**. Oral contraception is the most reliable method of non-surgical birth control. By altering the body's natural hormone balance, the pill interferes with the woman's normal monthly cycle of ovulation and menstruation and suppresses fertility. The pill is easy to use and does not interfere with lovemaking, but is not recommended for forgetful people.

Calendar method. This involves monitoring body temperature changes, cervical mucus consistency, and other body signs to pinpoint the fertile days. This is also known as the sympto-thermal method. All these methods are fairly unreliable and perhaps of more use to couples wanting to get pregnant than those trying not to.

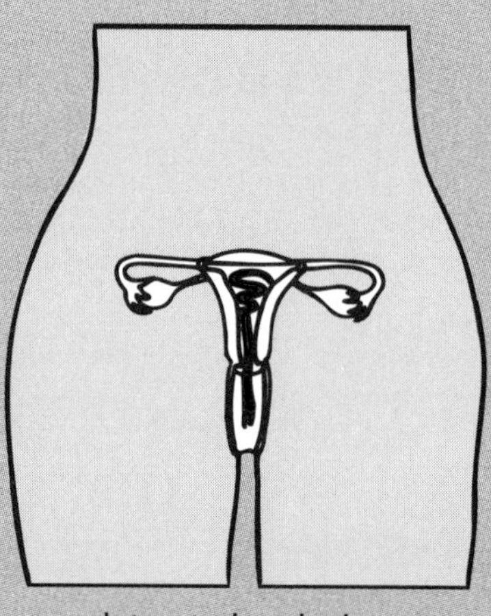

Intrauterine device (IUD, loop, coil)

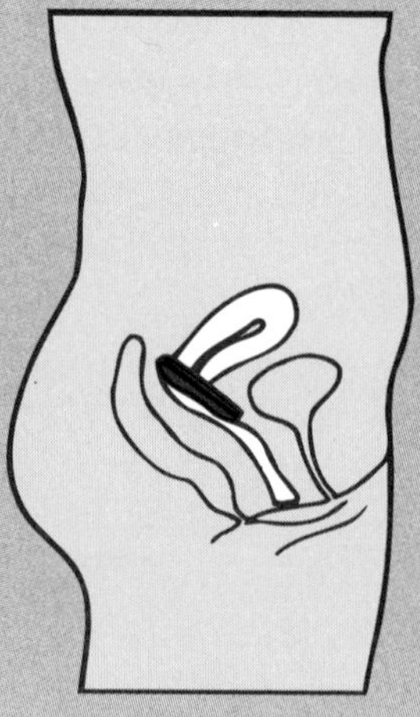

Diaphragm or cap

Morning-after pill. This is available as an emergency measure. It prevents implantation of a fertilized egg into the uterine lining.

Injections of slow-releasing hormones.

Implantation of slow releasing hormone capsules.

Intrauterine device (IUD) to prevent the fertilized egg from establishing a pregnancy. IUDs are nearly as efficient as the pill, are very convenient, and do not interfere with lovemaking. They need to be fitted by a doctor Complications include perforation of the uterus, ectopic pregnancy (a pregnancy that occurs outside the uterus), miscarriage if pregnancy occurs, abdominal pain, backache (often a sign of infection), and heavy periods. Expulsion of the IUD is also a possible problem. Users should regularly check that the tail threads are in the vagina.

Female sterilization. This is achieved by cutting or blocking the fallopian tubes, which prevents the eggs' normal journey from the ovaries to the uterus and their possible fertilization by sperm. Sterilization is reliable but is rarely reversible.

Diaphragm or **cap**. Used together with spermicide, a diaphragm or cap provides a barrier to sperm. The cap must always be used with spermicide, which is smeared on before inserting into the upper vagina, and it should be left in position for at least six hours following intercourse.

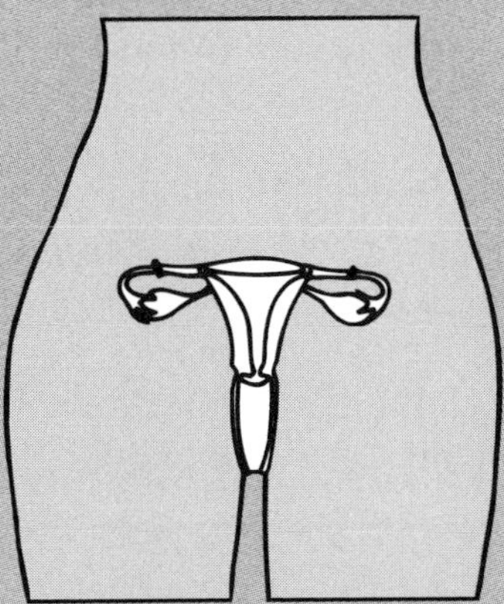

Female sterilization

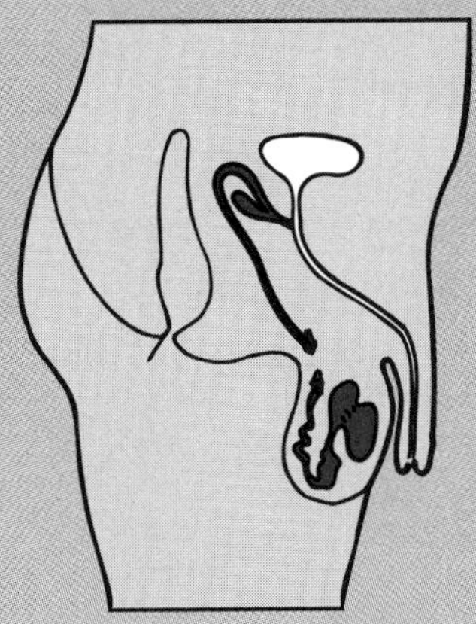

Male sterilization (vasectomy)

Condom. A condom fits tightly over an erect penis so that ejaculated sperm is trapped inside. Condoms are cheap, have no side-effects, and give protection against sexually transmitted diseases.

Coitus interruptus or withdrawal. This involves removal of the penis before ejaculation. This is highly unreliable.

Male sterilization or **vasectomy**. This involves cutting and tying the vas deferentia. The man continues to ejaculate but the semen no longer includes sperm.

Choice of contraceptive

The choice of contraceptive will be influenced by individual needs. Teenagers or young adults at the start of sexual activity often use withdrawal or condoms. Once sexual activity is established many young women use the pill, but concern about the side-effects of pill hormones may persuade others to choose one of the IUDs developed for women who have not had children. Between children some women continue using the pill or an IUD; others change to the slightly less effective diaphragm. Once the family is complete, some couples opt for sterilization of either the man or the woman.

© DIAGRAM

The inability to conceive can be a source of great unhappiness and anxiety for couples. As a general guideline, if a couple who want children have been having sex regularly without contraception for more than a year and the woman has not become pregnant, they should seek medical advice. There may be a simple solution to the problem. For example, by combining knowledge about the likely time of a woman's ovulation with information about the life span of sperm inside a woman, it becomes possible to predict those times of the month when she is most likely to conceive. Some couples can increase the likelihood of conception by using a different intercourse position.

Other causes of failure to become pregnant may be due to stress, physical problems, or infections. The most common causes are highlighted here and on pages 90–91.

Female physical problems

As in men there may be hormone disorders and defects of the central nervous system. Other problem sites are shown on the diagram (right).

1 Cervix: infection, injury, or the presence of fibrous growths (endometriosis) cause pain.

2 Uterus: there may be pain; fertility may be affected if the uterus is tilted, divided, or double.

3 Vagina: causes of pain on intercourse include infection, lack of lubrication, slackness or tightness of the vaginal walls, sensitivity to rubber devices, and vaginismus.

4 Vaginal outlet: labia fused over the outlet prevent intercourse; pain may result from a very rigid hymen, from atrophy due to aging, or from injury associated with first intercourse, IUD strings, rape, abortion, or childbirth.

5 Ovaries: ovulatory problems are a cause of infertility; pain on intercourse may be due to inflammation, displacement or ovarian cysts.

6 Fallopian tubes: infection may cause pain on intercourse; blockage of the tubes is a common cause of infertility.

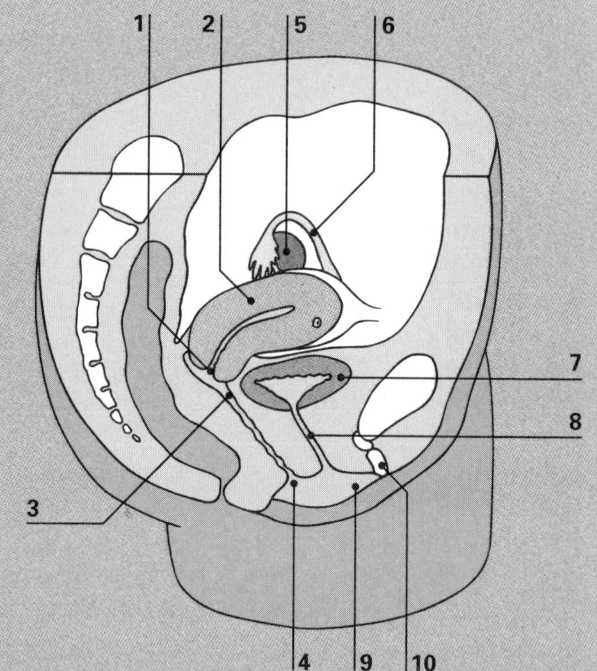

7 Bladder: infection is a cause of painful intercourse.

8 Urethra: infection is a cause of painful intercourse.

9 Vulva: atrophy in old age may make intercourse painful.

10 Clitoris: smegma, infection, and injury are causes of pain during intercourse.

Male physical problems

The sites of some possible problems involving the male sex organs are located on the drawing (below).

1 Seminal vesicles: infection causes pain on intercourse; the production of too much or too little seminal fluid are causes of infertility.

2 Prostate gland: infection, over-enlargement, cancer and, in older men, spasmodic contractions are causes of pain during intercourse.

3 Compressor muscles: failure of these muscles to relax at ejaculation causes seminal fluid to be discharged into the bladder instead of being discharged through the urethra. This problem—termed retrograde ejaculation—may result from prostate surgery or an accident.

4 Bladder: infection causes pain on intercourse.

5 Urethra: adhesions following gonorrheal infection cause pain on intercourse.

6 Testes: failure of the testes to descend before puberty causes infertility, as does inadequate production of sperm; painful intercourse can result from unrelieved congestion of the testes following prolonged erection without ejaculation.

7 Blood vessels: hardening of blood vessels leading to the erectile tissue of the penis means that older men take longer to obtain an erection.

8 Shaft of the penis: pain on intercourse may be the result of a badly performed circumcision, or may be caused by Peyronie's disease (in which the penis on erection is painfully bowed up or sideways) or by chordee (in which the erect penis is painfully bowed down).

9 Glans: pain in the glans during intercourse may be caused by a build-up of smegma and bacteria, by adhesion of the glans to an overtight foreskin, by inflammation of the urethra or prostate, or by contact with germs, acid, or a partner's contraceptive cream.

Other physical problems that interfere with male sexual performance include disorders of hormone production in the pituitary or the testes, and defects of the central nervous system.

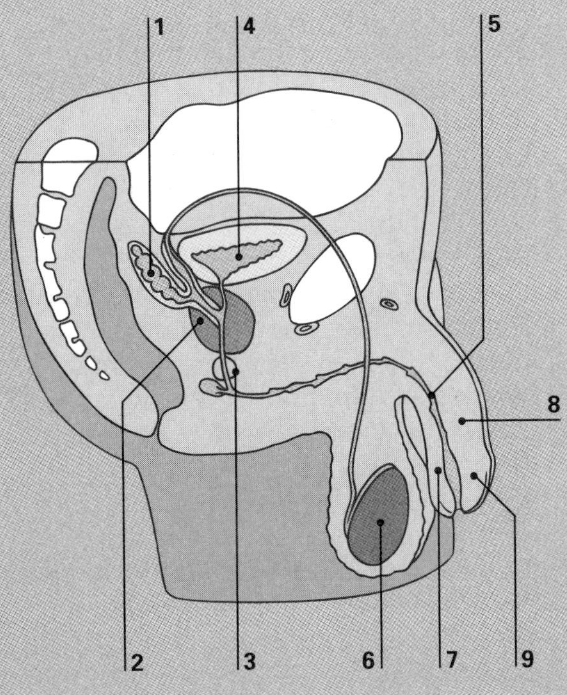

© DIAGRAM

Sexual infections

Although modern medicine can cure most sexually transmitted diseases (STDs), annual numbers of cases remain alarmingly high. In the U.S. there are more than 360,000 new cases of gonorrhea reported each year, and more than three million people may be infected with chlamydia annually. Meanwhile new cases of AIDS in the U.S. exceed 42,000 each year and there may be more than 45 million Americans infected with the genital herpes virus. Hindrances in the eradication of sexual diseases include increased promiscuity, global travel by sexually active individuals if combined with a failure to use condoms, and the appearance of new strains of disease that resist drugs and have symptom-free carriers.

Symptoms and treatments

- **Candidiasis** (thrush): women have an itchy, swollen vulva, curdy vaginal discharge, and pain during coitus and urination; men may have a red, spotty penis and inner foreskin, with a burning sensation. Treatment is with fungicide.
- **Chlamydia**: this is a bacterial infection that causes discharge from the penis and pain on urination; women may have increased vaginal discharge, pain on urination, and abdominal pain. It is treated with antibiotics. If left untreated, it can cause infertility.
- **Crab lice**: these produce itching in areas covered by pubic or other body hair. Special lotions cure the problem.
- **Genital herpes**: four to five days after infection itchy blisters appear on the genitals and then burst to produce ulcers. All symptoms go away in two weeks but milder attacks may recur. As yet there is no cure.
- **Genital warts**: appearing one to six months after infection, these form a tiny "cauliflower" around genitals or anus. Caustic substances, freezing, or cauterization remove them.
- **Gonorrhea**: first symptoms in men, usually 210 days after infection, are a watery (later thicker, greenish-yellow) penile discharge, frequent urge to urinate and pain on urination; only 20 percent of females infected show early symptoms—a red, raw vulva, white, yellow or green vaginal discharge, and perhaps pain on urination. Treatment is with antibiotics.
- **HIV** (human immunodeficiency virus): The cause of AIDS (acquired immunodeficiency syndrome), a fatal condition that destroys the body's immune system. There is no cure.
- **Scabies**: small itchy lumps and thin dark lines caused by mites.
- **Syphilis**: in the first month a small painless sore appears on the part directly infected. About two months after infection there is a skin rash and patchy hair loss, lasting up to a year. The symptoms then disappear, but may return up to 30 years after infection, when organs are damaged.
- **Trichomoniasis**: symptoms in women are a foul-smelling, greenish, foamy vaginal discharge, and inflammation of the vagina and vulva; men usually have no symptoms but can transmit the disease. Treatment is by drugs.

Disease prevention

The following precautions reduce the risk of genital infection:

- Wash genitals daily.
- Change underwear daily.
- Avoid underwear made of nylon as this tends to harbor germs.
- Avoid contact with chemicals that irritate the genitals.
- Wipe the bottom from front to back at toilet visits to avoid transferring germs from the anus to the urethra.
- Keep sexual contact to one infection-free partner.
- Leave six weeks between sexual partners in order to reduce your risk of unknowingly incubating a sexual infection that might be passed on.
- Look for discharge or sores on a new partner's genitals.
- Use a condom during intercourse. Contraceptive creams and foams also help to block some infections.
- Wash genitals before and after intercourse.
- Urinate after intercourse.

Early treatment of sexually transmitted disease is essential. The following measures should prevent serious complications developing:

- If you suspect you have a sexually transmitted disease, have a confidential medical examination as soon as possible.
- Advise your partner to seek medical aid.
- Avoid sexual contact.
- Follow the treatment prescribed.
- Have a repeat test to make sure you are cured.

The aging female

Although menopause ends a woman's reproductive potential, any loss of sex drive at this time is usually temporary. In fact women usually find that their cycle of sexual response is less affected by age than is that of their partner. The postmenopausal changes listed here may make intercourse uncomfortable for some women, but hormone pills and local applications are available to alleviate their effects. **1** The vulva atrophies. **2** The vaginal walls get thinner; reduced lubrication may lead to vaginal irritation. **3** Ovaries shrink. **4** The uterus shrinks; uterine muscle becomes fibrous but is probably still contractile.

The aging male

Most older men remain physically capable of sexual activity. Impotence does increase with age, but in most cases this is due to psychological causes. By about age 60, however, aging will have brought the following physical changes. **1** Hardening of blood vessels affects erectile capacity. **2** Scrotal tissue sags and wrinkles. **3** Testes shrink, lose firmness, and are less elevated on arousal. **4** Thickening and degeneration of the seminiferous tubules inhibit sperm production. **5** The prostate gland may be enlarged and its contractions during orgasm are weaker. **6** Seminal fluid is thinner and reduced in quantity.

© DIAGRAM

Most babies are born after a gestation period of between 38 and 42 weeks. During a natural birth the baby travels from the uterus through the vagina, or birth canal, into the outside world. This process is called labor. Labor is very painful and can last a few hours or even two or three days.

Labor facts

- Most babies are born head first.
- The head is the largest part of the newborn baby.

How sex is determined

Female cells contain two X chromosomes. Male cells have an X and a Y chromosome.

1 A male produces sperm which contains, with equal probability, either an X or a Y chromosome. A female produces ova which always carry an X chromosome.

2 When a sperm and ovum fuse at fertilization, the sex of the resulting child is determined by the type of sex chromosome passed on in the sperm.

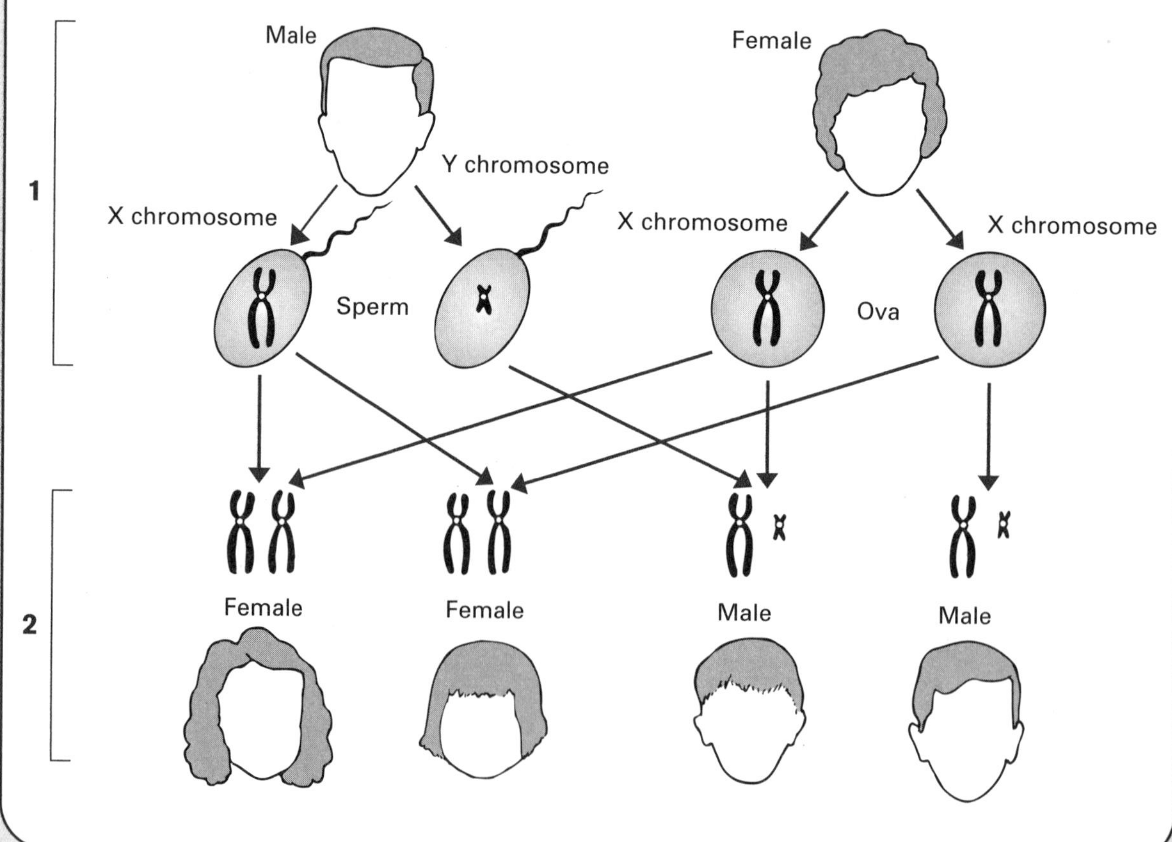

First stage of labor

Most labors follow a similar general pattern. In the first stage, the cervix of the uterus "effaces" and dilates (widens) to allow the fetus to pass without damaging it. The process takes about eight hours for women having their first baby and about four to five hours for subsequent babies. Contractions become stronger and more frequent through this stage.

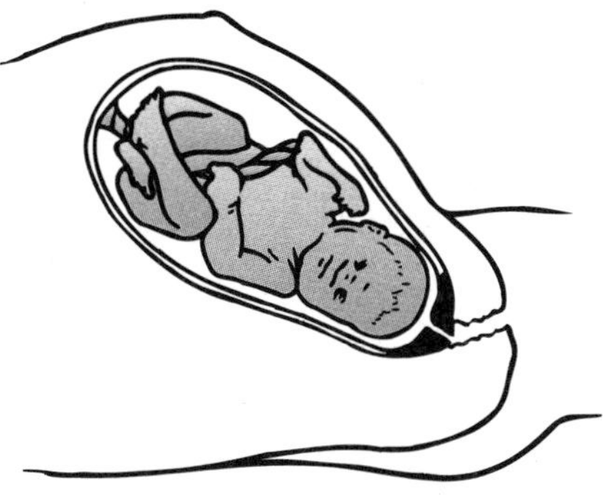

1 Partial effacement
Contraction and retraction of the uterus shorten the neck of the cervix. Contractions occur every ten minutes.

2 Full effacement
Contractions every five minutes. Pain is now felt abdominally.

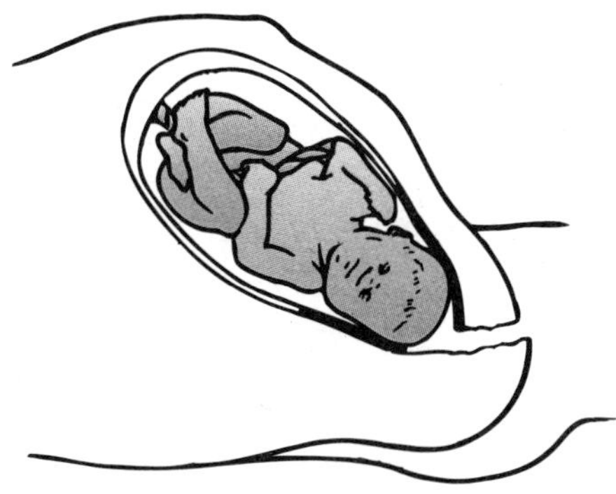

3 Partial dilation
Continued contraction and retraction. Contractions every two to five minutes. Amniotic sac ruptures (if not earlier).

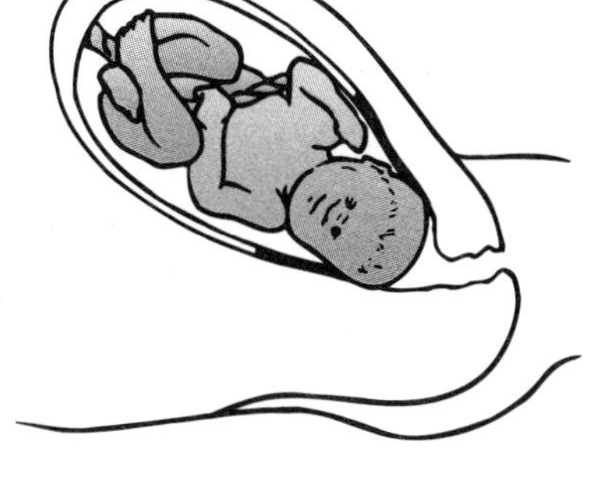

4 Full dilation
The fetus is able to pass through the cervix without damaging it. Contractions every two to three minutes.

© DIAGRAM

Second stage of labor

Transition to the second stage is characterized by feelings of pressure in the lower pelvis, backache, and often nausea, and leg cramps. There is a strong desire to bear down, and it is safe to do so once the cervix is fully dilated. The baby is now pushed out of the uterus and down the vagina, and will be delivered in anything from five to 40 minutes.

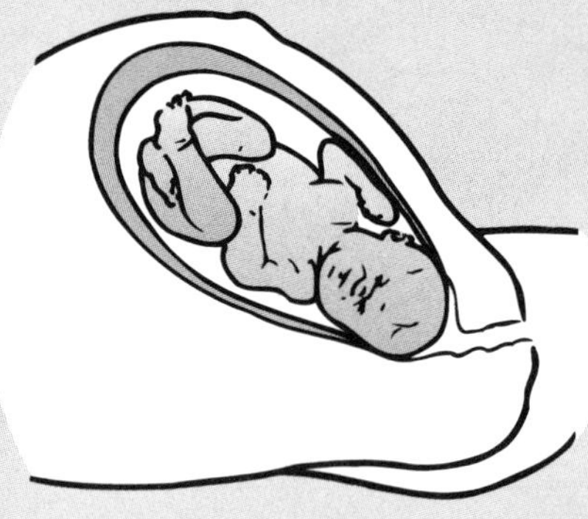

1 Full dilation marks the beginning of delivery. The woman "bears down" to help expel the baby.

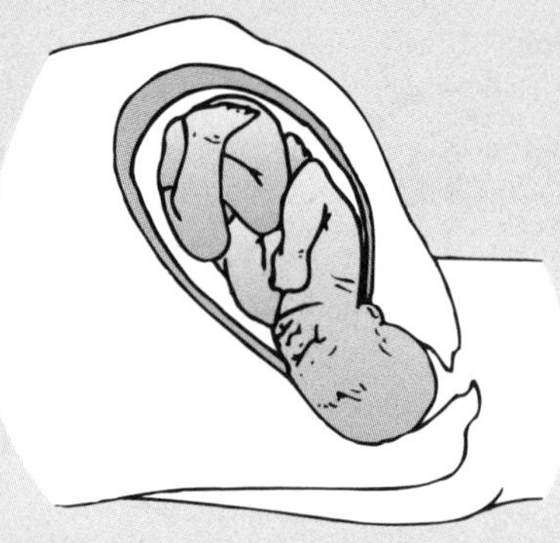

2 The baby's head passes through the cervix and rotates to squeeze beneath the pubic arch.

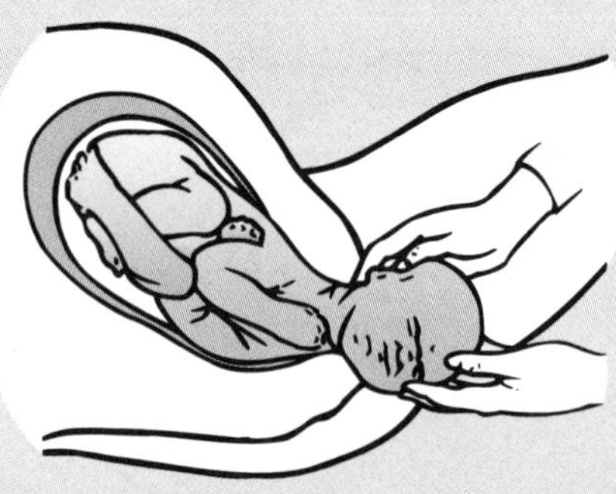

3 The head is born, and rotates back to its previous position. The baby's shoulders rotate to pass through the pelvis.

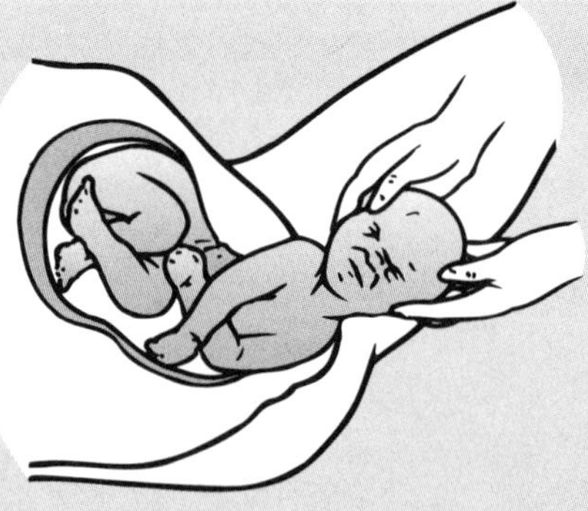

4 The right shoulder, then the left, is born. The baby starts breathing. Mucus is cleaned from its face and airways. The umbilical cord is clamped.

Third stage of labor

This final stage involves the delivery of the placenta. Hormones cause this to become detached from the endometrium and it is generally delivered within 30 minutes of the baby. Often the mother is given a hormone injection to hasten this process. If the placenta does not detach, it must be removed surgically.

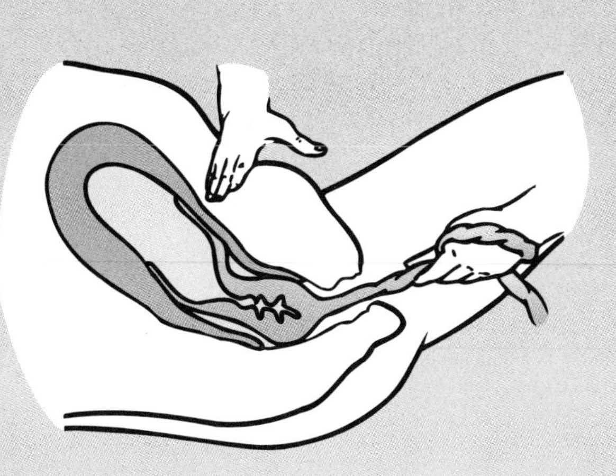

Fetal circulation after birth

At birth the newborn baby is still connected to the mother by the umbilical cord. This cord is clamped to stem the flow of blood between the two. The link between the umbilical vein and the newborn's blood supply breaks and the blood drains into the liver. The pulmonary vessels begin to carry blood to and from the lungs.

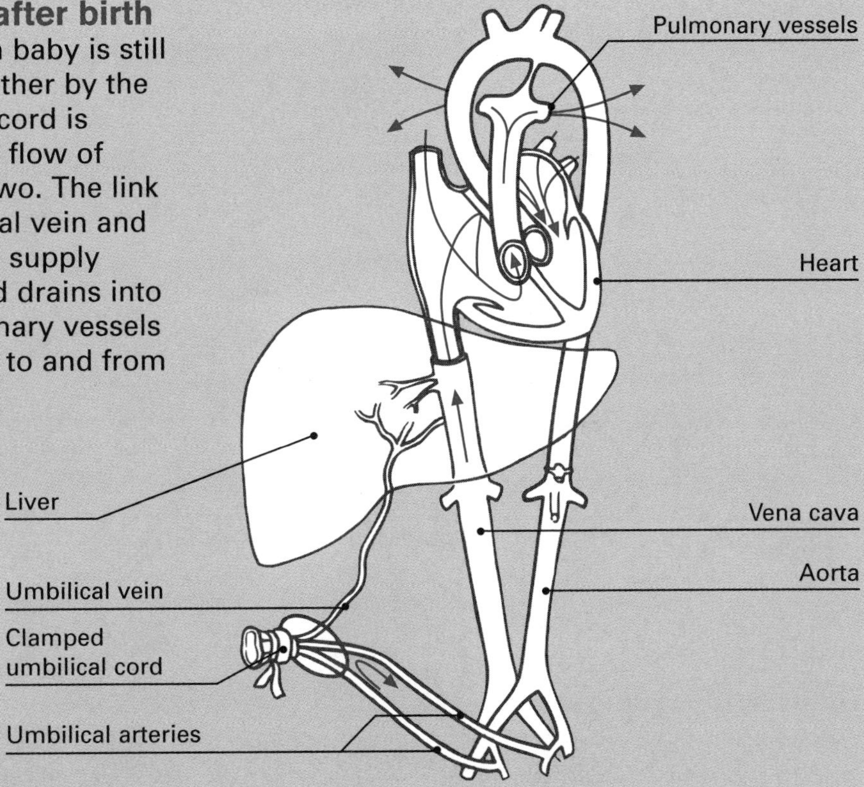

Pulmonary vessels
Heart
Liver
Vena cava
Aorta
Umbilical vein
Clamped umbilical cord
Umbilical arteries

© DIAGRAM

Fetal positions

Most babies are head down just before birth. The next most common position is breech. One percent of babies are transverse, while half as many are face down. Midwives use their hands to feel how the baby is positioned before birth.

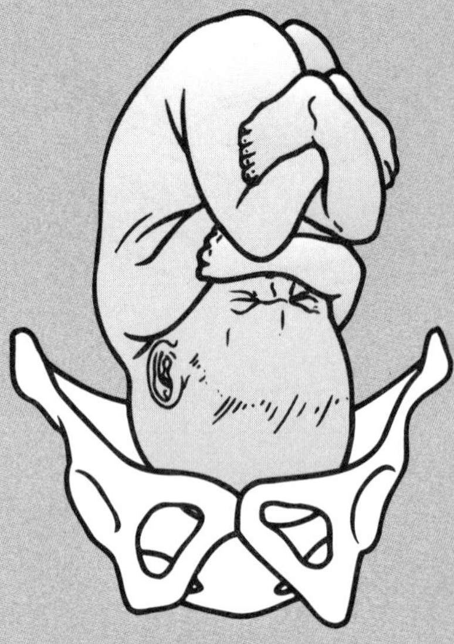

Vertex: head down

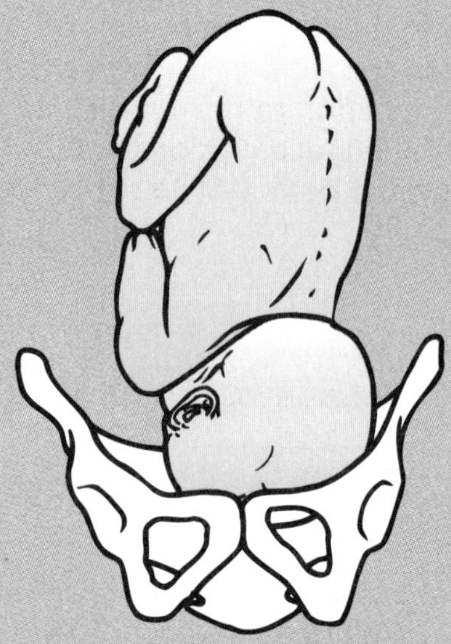

Vertex: face down

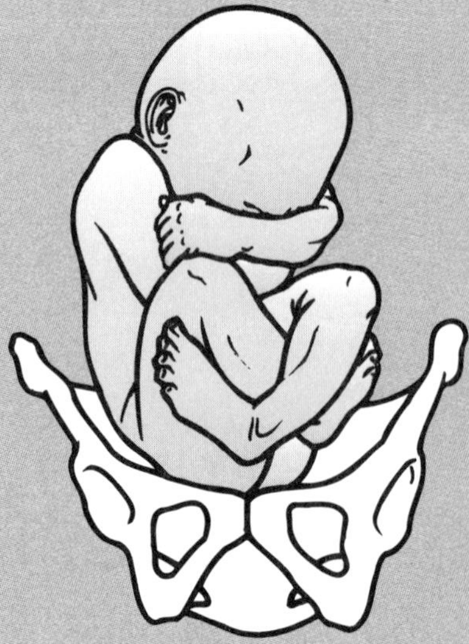

Breech

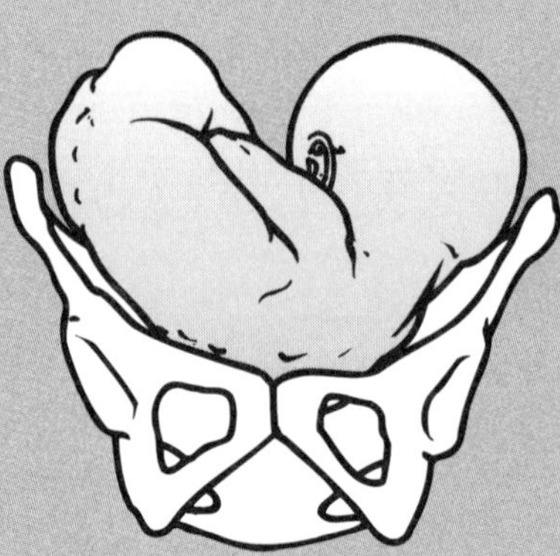

Transverse

Breech birth

Normally the fetus moves from breech to vertex position between the 24th and 28th week. However, some fail to do so, and 3.5 percent of fetuses remain breech (**a**) until birth. A normal-sized baby in breech position will usually be delivered with no problems for mother or child. But a small pelvis or a large fetal head may lead to difficulty. The duration of delivery can be critical. A long delivery may result in oxygen starvation if the head squeezes the umbilical cord. During a breech delivery the bottom passes through the cervix and rotates (**b**) to squeeze under the pubic arch. The bottom and legs are born first (**c**), then the shoulders, then the head.

Stages in a breech delivery

a

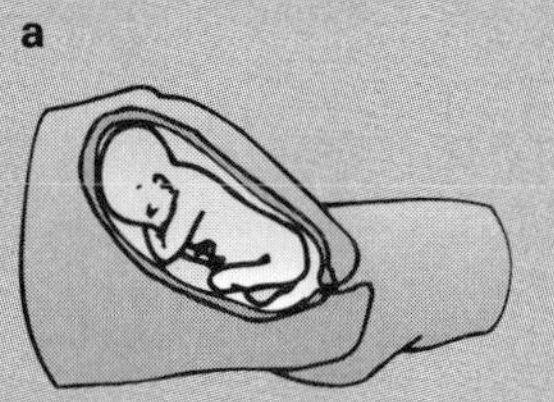

b

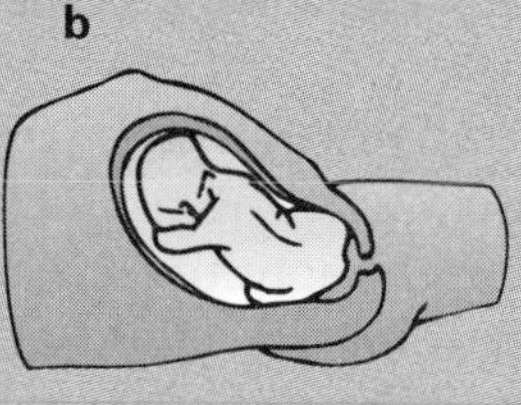

c

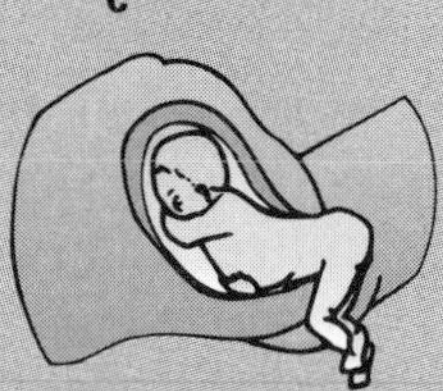

Forceps delivery

Forceps are sometimes used in the second stage of labor to aid delivery because of:

- slow or no fetal progress;
- maternal distress exacerbated by the effort required; or
- fetal distress.

Forceps have two curved blades that fit around the fetal head. One blade is inserted into the uterus and located in position around the head. The other blade is inserted, and locked into the first blade (**1**). Gentle traction then draws the fetus through the vagina (**2**).

Stages in a forceps delivery

1

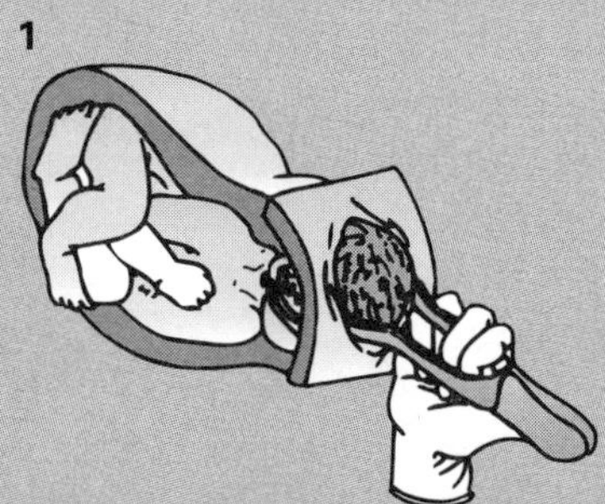

2

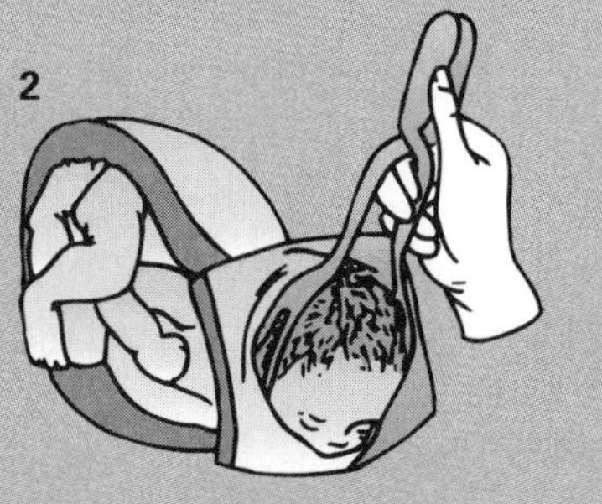

Cesarean birth

Cesarean section is an operation carried out on a pregnant woman to deliver her baby if this is not possible through the vagina. Reasons for this include:

- fetal distress;
- a placenta lying over the cervical opening;
- very small pelvis;
- obstructive fibroids;
- transverse fetal position; or
- previous uterine injury.

A general anesthetic is given. A cut is made below the navel into the abdomen and uterus, and the baby is delivered through this.

© DIAGRAM

During the first week of life, a baby is not capable of any significant voluntary or controlled movements. However, it does exhibit a variety of reflexes—involuntary or automatic reactions to particular changes in its surroundings or to touch. These "primitive" reflexes are thought to be a legacy of humanity's earliest ancestors, when such actions were vital for an infant's survival.

Development of a baby's muscle control starts from the head and moves gradually downward to the arms, legs, and feet. Within a week, from a cradled position a baby can move its head up for a second or two , and by a month it can balance its head for several seconds, provided the rest of its body is supported. By this time, too, it can stretch out its limbs and fan out its fingers and toes.

Vital statistics

Newborn babies vary greatly in size and weight but on average measure:

- 19.9 inches (50.5 cm) in length
- 7.5 pounds (3.4 kg) in weight and, after an initial loss of weight, by three months measure:
- 23.6 inches (59.8 cm) in length
- weigh 12.5 pounds (5.7 kg)

Newborn reflexes

A newborn's reflexes last for several days then fade. The physical abilities are re-learned months later.

1 Rooting reflex If one side of a baby's cheek or mouth is gently touched, the baby will turn its head in the direction of the touch. This ensures that the baby will seek out its mother's nipple when its cheek is brushed by her breast. Along with the sucking and swallowing reflexes, the rooting reflex is essential for successful feeding of the newborn.

2 Neck reflex When on its back and not crying, a newborn baby turns its head to one side, the arm on that side extends as shown, and the opposite leg bends at the knee.

3 Grasp reflex If an object is placed in the baby's hand, it clenches its fist. If a finger is slipped into each of its palms, the baby will grasp them so tightly that it can support its own weight.

1

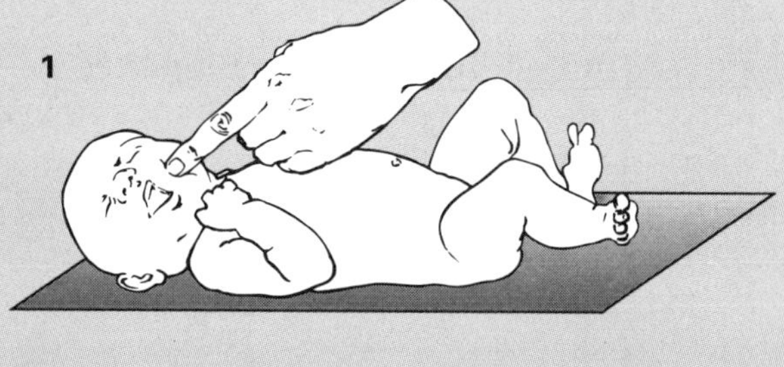

2

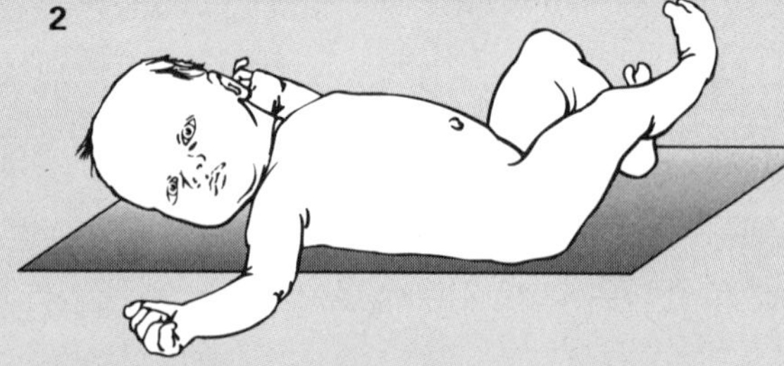

3

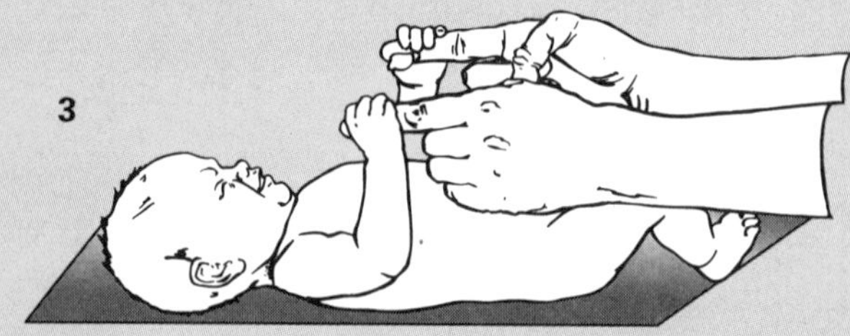

Growth pattern

Babies do not all grow and develop at the same rate. Growth depends on a mixture of diet, health, metabolism, functioning of glands, and genetic factors. Also, babies that are born prematurely have a great deal of catching up to do. For example, a baby born after a pregnancy of only eight months will still be a month behind a full-term baby six months later. However, a baby's weight will have roughly doubled after six months, and by a year its height will have increased from about 20 inches (50 cm) to 30 inches (75 cm). On average, at birth boys are longer and taller than girls and stay ahead until the age of about four or five years.

Proportions

Compared to an adult, a newborn baby's head is relatively large and its legs are comparatively short. At first, the legs and arms grow quickly. Then the whole body elongates. By about two years, a child reaches half its adult height. It is not until the age of about six or seven that a child is properly proportioned.

4 Moro reflex This reflex is seen when the baby is startled. The arms and legs are oustretched and then drawn inward with the fingers curled as if ready to clutch at something. A baby's Moro reflex is tested to check muscle tone—if the limbs respond asymmetrically, there may be an injury or weakness of a particular limb.
5 Stepping reflex If the front of the baby's legs are brought into contact with the edge of a table, the baby will raise its legs and take a step up onto the table.
6 Walking reflex If a baby is held upright with the soles of its feet on a flat surface, and is then moved forward slowly, it will respond with walking steps.

Other reflexes include blinking in response to a stimulus such as touching the baby on the bridge of the nose and, when the baby is lying down, drawing one leg up toward its body when the sole of the foot on the other leg is stroked.

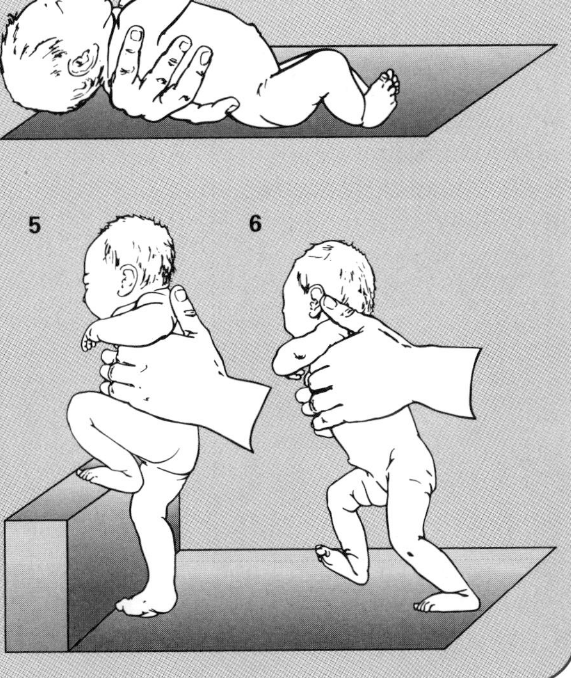

© DIAGRAM

Child development

Six months old

At this age, babies still cannot sit or stand unaided. They can use their hands well and continually handle and bang objects. They are now learning the meaning of people's expressions and gestures, and react with two-syllabled sounds.

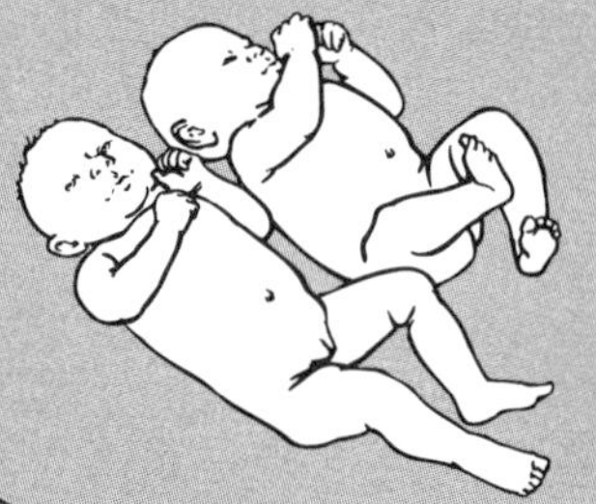

One year old

Agile crawling has given mobility, and babies can now nearly stand and walk unaided. They love to imitate actions and start to speak.

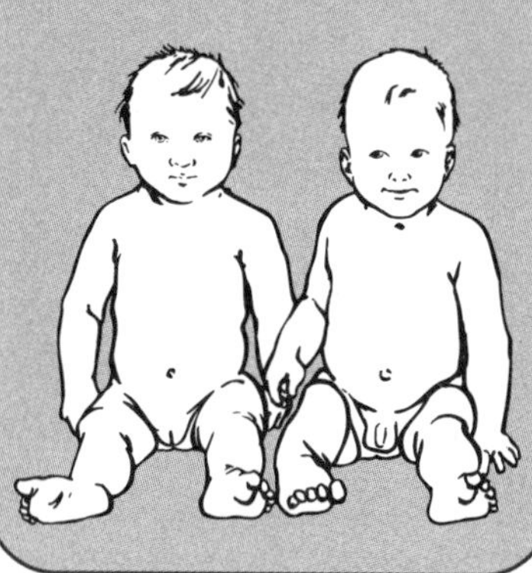

18 months old

Having learned to stand, walk, and run, young children—now often called infants—are immensely active. But they cannot easily coordinate their hands and feet. They are dexterous, but lack wrist control. Their use of words is very limited. Self-willed, they take but cannot give and, unable to see other people like themselves, they cannot share in their play.

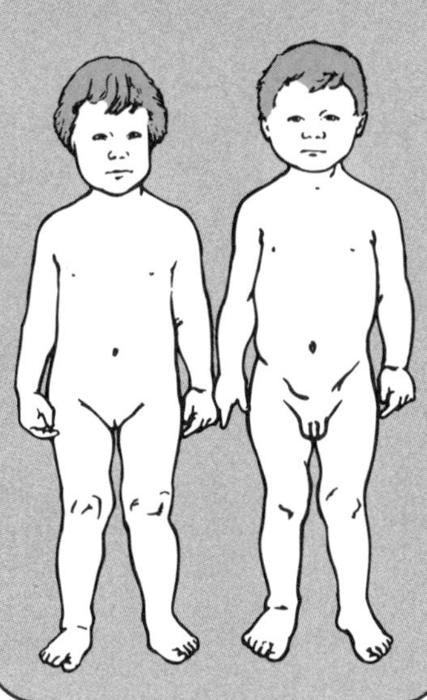

Two years old

Young children are now referred to as toddlers—they are surer on their feet, and love to romp, chase, and be pursued, but sometimes fall over. Rising and bending down are still done somewhat awkwardly. Hand movements are now more varied and assured. They love exploring objects, testing everything by taste and touch. They can speak many words clearly.

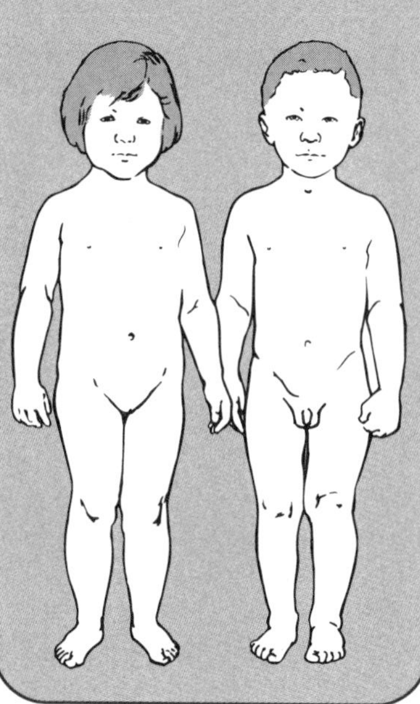

Four years old

Well-controlled muscles help youngsters energetically jump, hop, skip, climb, and ride a tricycle. Their hand-eye coordination is well developed, allowing them, for example, to draw, lace their shoes, and cut with scissors. They talk incessantly, trying out new words and using adult terms out of context. Their mental life is blossoming.

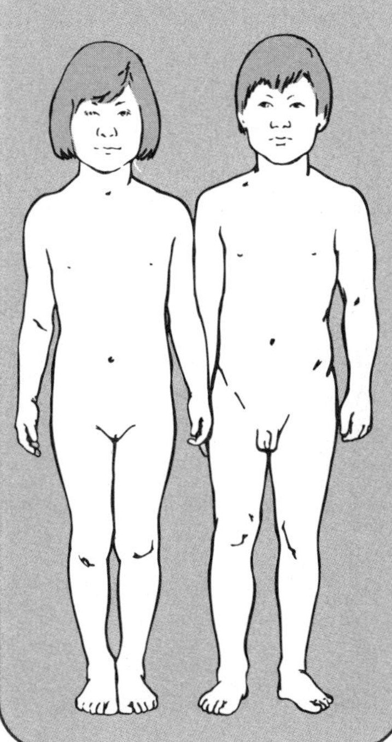

Six years old

Lively, expansive, and eager, six-year-olds have an insatiable appetite for fresh experiences. Many youngsters are now demanding, stubborn, and unruly. At school, they take their first steps in reading, writing, and using numbers. But what they learn must still be firmly based on things they can see and do. They cannot reason in an adult abstract way.

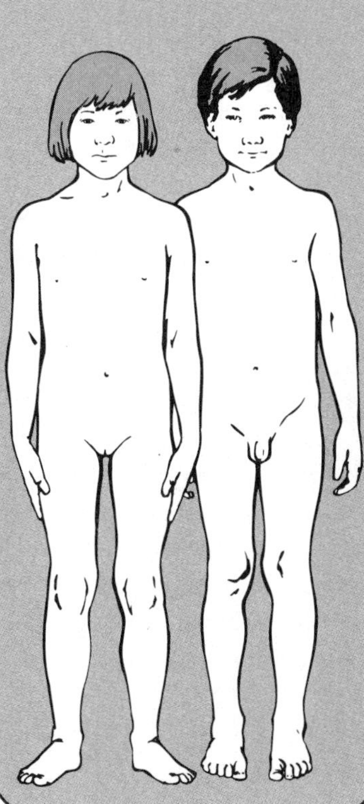

Eight years old

Physically, children now have adult body proportions and believe no task or action is beyond their capabilities. Their vocabulary is enriched by many adjectives because they now appreciate the qualities of objects and actions. They have a new, maturing independence and start to show what sort of people they will become.

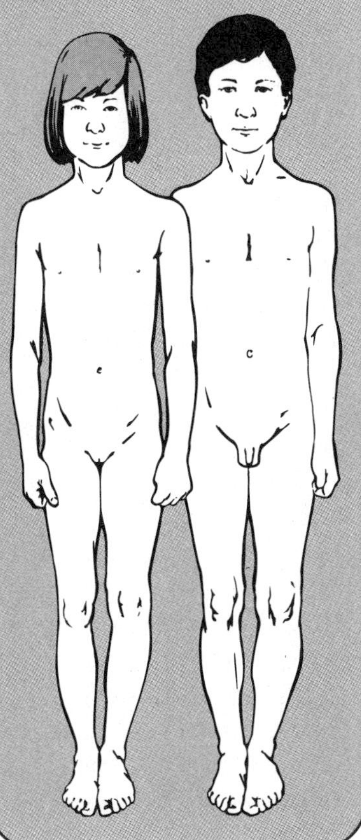

© DIAGRAM

Glossary of the human body

Adipose tissue Connective tissue containing numerous fat cells.
Adrenal glands (*or* Suprarenal glands) Endocrine glands located on each kidney. The cortex and medulla produce a range of hormones.
Afferent Directed toward a central organ or part of the body.
Alimentary canal (*or* Gastrointestinal tract *or* Gut) The digestive tract: a tube starting at the mouth and ending at the anus.
Anus The lower end of the rectum, forming the outlet of the alimentary canal.
Aorta The largest artery, arising from the left ventricle of the heart.
Appendix (*or* Vermiform appendix) A short, wormlike tube opening into the cecum but closed at the other end. It contains lymphoid tissue, which is involved in immunity.
Arteriole A small artery supplying blood from a main artery to a capillary.
Artery A blood vessel transporting blood from the heart to elsewhere in the body.
Atrioventricular valve (*or* AV valve) A valve between a ventricle and an atrium. The right atrioventricular valve (*or* tricuspid valve) has three cusps. The left atrioventricular valve (mitral valve or bicuspid valve) has two cusps.
Auditory Relating to hearing.
Axillary Relating to the armpit.
Backbone *See* **Vertebral column**.
Basal ganglia Paired structures deep in the forebrain: they help coordinate and control willed muscle movements.
Basophil A type of white blood cell that is readily stained by basic dyes.
Biceps A muscle with two heads: biceps brachii in the upper arm and biceps femoris in the thigh.
Bile ducts Tiny tubes that carry bile (a liver secretion) from the liver to the duodenum.
Bladder A sac, especially the muscular bag inside the pelvis where urine collects before being expelled from the body.
Blood A sticky red fluid consisting of colorless plasma, red blood cells (Erythrocytes), white blood cells (Leukocytes), and platelets (thrombocytes).
Blood pressure The pressure of blood against blood-vessel walls, especially artery walls.
Bone The hard, dense connective tissue that forms the skeleton's components.
Bone marrow Soft red and yellow substances that fill cavities in bone.
Bowel *See* **Large intestine**.
Brain The body's chief control center, consisting of billions of interconnected nerve cells.
Brainstem A stalklike part of the brain, between the cerebrum and spinal cord. It contains the midbrain, pons, and medulla oblongata.
Breast A female breast consists mainly of a mammary (milk-secreting) gland embedded in fatty tissue.
Breastbone *See* **Sternum**.
Bronchiole A small subdivision of a bronchus, ending in tiny air sacs called alveoli.
Bronchus The main tubes branching from the lower end of the trachea and forming the main airways to and from the lungs (plural: bronchi).
Capillary The tiniest type of blood vessel, connecting an arteriole and a venule.
Cardiac Relating to the heart.
Cardiovascular Relating to the heart and blood circulatory system.
Cartilage Gristle: dense, white connective tissue cushioning bones.
Cecum The first part of the large intestine, forming a blind pouch.
Cell The basic unit of the body, usually comprising an outer membrane, cytoplasm, a nucleus, and organelles.

Central nervous system (CNS) The brain and spinal cord.
Cerebellum The largest part of the hindbrain. It helps coordinate muscular movements.
Cerebral cortex The cerebrum's thin outer layer of gray matter.
Cerebral hemisphere Either of the two halves of the cerebrum.
Cerebrospinal fluid A clear fluid filling the brain's ventricles and surrounding the brain and spinal cord to protect them from injury.
Cerebrum The upper, major part of the brain, comprising cerebral hemispheres and diencephalon.
Cervix A neck, especially the neck of the uterus (womb) where it opens into the vagina.
Clavicle Either of the two collarbones.
Clitoris An erectile, pea-sized organ above the opening of the vagina; it is highly sensitive and is involved in female sexual response.
CNS *See* **Central nervous system**.
Coccyx Four fused vertebrae forming the "tail" of the backbone.
Collagen A fibrous protein that is a major constituent of connective tissue.
Colon The part of the large intestine between the cecum and rectum.
Connective tissue Tissue that supports, binds, or separates more specialized body tissues or acts as packing.
Corium *See* **Dermis**.
Cornea The transparent circular area at the front of the eye, which acts as a lens.
Coronary arteries Supply the heart muscle.
Corpuscles A term often used for red and white blood cells.
Cortex The outer layer of the brain.
Cranial nerves Twelve pairs of nerves linking the underside of the brain with parts of the head, neck, and thorax.
Cranium The part of the skull that contains the brain.
Cutaneous Relating to the skin.
Cuticle *See* **Epidermis**.
Deoxyribonucleic acid (DNA) A nucleic acid in the cell's chromosomes containing the cell's coded genetic instructions.
Dermis (*or* Corium) The layer of skin below the epidermis, containing nerves, blood vessels, glands, and hair follicles.
Diaphragm A muscular sheet used in breathing. It separates the thorax (chest) and abdomen (belly).
Digestion The chemical and mechanical breakdown of foods into substances that can be absorbed by the body.
DNA *See* **Deoxyribonucleic acid**.
Duodenum The upper part of the small intestine, where most chemical digestion takes place.
Ejaculation The discharging of semen from the penis.
Endocardium The membrane that lines the heart and the heart valves.
Endothelium The cell layer that lines the inside of the heart, blood vessels, and lymph vessels.
Enzymes Biological catalysts: proteins that speed up chemical reactions without undergoing change themselves.
Epidermis (*or* Cuticle) The skin's outer layer.
Epiglottis A cartilage flap behind the tongue that is closed during swallowing to stop food from entering the larynx.
Epiphysis *See* **Pineal gland**.
Epithelium The cell layer covering the body, and lining the alimentary canal and respiratory and urinary tracts.
Erythrocytes Red blood cells.
Esophagus (*or* Gullet) The muscular tube through which food travels between the pharynx and the stomach.

© DIAGRAM

Fallopian tubes (*or* Uterine tubes *or* Oviducts) The tubes through which ova (eggs) travel from the ovaries to the uterus.
Femur The thigh bone: the long bone between the hip and the knee.
Follicle A small secreting cavity or sac. Ova (egg cells) develop in follicles in the female ovaries.
Forebrain The front part of the brain comprising diencephalon and telencephalon.
Gallbladder A pear-shaped bag where bile is stored, below the liver.
Gametes Sex cells: sperm in males; ova in females.
Gastric Of the stomach.
Gastrointestinal tract *See* **Alimentary canal**.
Genes Basic biological hereditary units, consisting of DNA, located on chromosomes.
Genitalia Sex organs.
Gland A structure that synthesizes and secretes a fluid.
Gonads Primary reproductive organs: the ovaries and testes.
Granulocytes White blood cells with cytoplasm that contains granules: basophils, eosinophils, and monocytes.
Gray matter The darker tissue of the brain and spinal cord mainly consisting of neurons' cell bodies and dendrites.
Gullet *See* **Esophagus**.
Gut *See* **Alimentary canal**.
Heart The hollow, muscular, fist-sized organ that pumps blood around the body.
Hemoglobin The iron-rich, oxygen-transporting pigment in red blood cells that gives them their color.
Hepatic Relating to the liver.
Hepatic portal vein *See* **Portal vein**.
Hindbrain Brain structures below the midbrain, comprising the pons, medulla oblongata, and cerebellum.
Hormones Chemical substances released into the blood by endocrine glands to influence organs or tissues in other parts of the body.
Hypophysis *See* **Pituitary gland**.
Hypothalamus A part of the brain with endocrine functions.
Ileum The last part of the small intestine.
Immune system The body's defense system against infective organisms or other foreign bodies. It includes the lymphatic system.
Involuntary muscle Muscle that is not under conscious control. *See also* **Smooth muscle**.
Jejunum The middle part of the small intestine.
Joint The junction between bones.
Karyotype The chromosome complement of a person or species: the genome.
Kidney A bean-shaped organ that filters wastes from blood to form urine.
Lactation Milk production by the mammary glands.
Large intestine (*or* Bowel) The lower part of the alimentary canal, comprising the cecum, colon, and rectum.
Larynx The cartilaginous voice box.
Leukocytes White blood cells. They attack invading microorganisms and help to combat injuries.
Ligament Fibrous tissue that connects bones.
Liver The largest organ in the body, it is involved in various metabolic processes.
Lungs The two organs of respiration, filling most of the chest cavity inside the rib cage and above the diaphragm.
Lymph A transparent fluid that leaks from blood vessels into tissue spaces.
Lymph gland *See* **Lymph node**.
Lymph node (*or* Lymph gland) One of the "knots" in the lymphatic system, which contain lymphocytes and macrophages that filter the lymph passing through the nodes.

Lymphatic system A network of lymph vessels and lymph nodes. Vessels collect lymph from body tissues and return it to the blood after harmful substances have been filtered out in the lymph nodes.
Mammary glands The milk-producing structures in the breast.
Medulla oblongata The lowest part of the brain stem, containing the vital centers that control heartbeat and respiration.
Meiosis A type of cell division that produces daughter cells (sperm and ova) each with half as many chromosomes as the parent cell.
Meninges Three protective membranes surrounding the brain and spinal cord.
Menopause When a woman ceases to have menstrual periods.
Menstruation Menstrual periods: the monthly flow of blood and uterine lining from the vagina of nonpregnant females of childbearing age.
Metabolism The array of continuous chemical changes that maintain life in the body.
Mitosis Ordinary cell division in which both daughter cells have as many chromosomes as the parent cell.
Mucous membranes The mucus-secreting linings of the digestive, respiratory, reproductive, and urinary tracts.
Nasal Relating to the nose.
Nasal cavity The space inside the nose between the base of the skull and the roof of the mouth.
Nerve A bundle of nerve fibers (axons) that transmit impulses to (in the case of sensory nerves) or from (in the case of motor nerves) the central nervous system.
Nervous system The coordinated networks of neurons that control the body. It is divided into the central nervous system (brain and spinal cord), and the peripheral nervous system (the somatic and autonomic nervous systems).
Neuron (*or* Neurone) A nerve cell: the basic unit of the nervous system.
Neurone *See* **Neuron**.
Neurotransmitter A chemical released at nerve endings to transmit nerve impulses across synapses.
Nucleic acids Molecules that store genetic information.
Nucleus The control center of a cell, which contains coded genetic instructions.
Olfactory Relating to smell.
Optic Relating to the eye.
Organ A body part with different types of tissue that performs a particular task.
Organelles Tiny structures (miniorgans) in a cell's cytoplasm with particular tasks.
Ovaries Female sex organs that produce ova (eggs) and sex hormones.
Oviducts *See* **Fallopian tubes**.
Ovulation The release of a ripe egg from a female's ovary.
Ovum An egg; a female sex cell (plural: ova).
Palate The roof of the mouth.
Pancreas An abdominal organ that produces pancreatic juice and the hormones glucagon and insulin.
Parasympathetic nervous system The part of the autonomic nervous system that predominates when the body is at rest.
Parathyroid glands Four pea-sized endocrine glands on the thyroid gland. They produce parathyroid hormone, which controls blood calcium level.
Pelvis A bony basin formed by the two hip bones, the sacrum, and the coccyx.
Pericardium The double-layered membrane that encloses the heart and attaches it to the diaphragm and sternum.
Peristalsis Waves of muscular contraction that propel substances through passageways, such as the alimentary canal.

© DIAGRAM

Phagocytes Types of leukocytes that engulf and destroy microorganisms and foreign bodies.
Pharynx The throat.
Pineal gland (*or* Epiphysis) An endocrine gland in the brain that secretes melatonin.
Pituitary gland (*or* Hypophysis) A three-lobed, pea-sized gland below the hypothalamus. It produces growth hormone, hormones that act on other endocrine glands, oxytocin, and ADH. It is often called the body's "master gland."
Plasma The fluid part of blood.
Pleura The membrane that covers the lungs (visceral pleura) and lines the chest wall (parietal pleura).
Plexus A network of nerves (or blood or lymph vessels).
Portal vein (*or* Hepatic portal vein) Drains blood from digestive organs to the liver.
Prostate gland A gland situated below the bladder in males. It produces a sperm-activating fluid that forms nearly a third of the semen's volume.
Pudendum *See* **Vulva**.
Pulmonary Relating to the lungs.
Receptor A structure, such as a sensory nerve ending, specialized to detect environmental stimuli.
Rectum The last part of the colon, where feces collects before leaving the body.
Reflex action The body's automatic response to a stimulus, such as blinking.
Renal Relating to the kidney.
Respiration 1) Breathing; 2) Taking in oxygen and giving out carbon dioxide; 3) Deriving energy from food with or without using oxygen.
Respiratory system In humans, the mouth, nose, pharynx, larynx, trachea, bronchi, bronchioles, alveoli, and lungs.
Ribonucleic acid (RNA) A nucleic acid concerned with protein synthesis.
Ribs Twelve pairs of bones that protect the chest cavity and assist breathing by moving up and out during inspiration and down and in during expiration.
Salivary glands The lingual, parotid, sublingual, and submandibular glands that produce saliva.
Serum Blood plasma that does not contain clotting factors but does contain antibodies.
Sinus A cavity, such as the channels draining venous blood from the brain.
Skeleton The bony framework that protects and supports the body's soft tissues.
Skin The body's waterproof covering; its largest organ, comprising two main layers: the epidermis and dermis.
Small intestine The alimentary canal between the stomach and large intestine, comprising the duodenum, jejunum, and ileum. Most digestion occurs here.
Smooth muscle (*or* Unstriated muscle *or* Involuntary muscle) Muscle without striped fibers that automatically operates internal organs such as the stomach, bladder, and blood vessels.
Sphincter A ring-shaped muscle that contracts to close an orifice.
Spinal cord The cable of nerve tissue running down inside the vertebral column (spine) and linking the brain with nerves supplying most of the body.
Spine *See* **Vertebral column**.
Sternum The breastbone.
Subcutaneous tissue The sheet of connective tissue below the dermis.
Suprarenal glands *See* **Adrenal glands**.
Suture An immovable fibrous joint between the skull bones.
Taste buds Tiny sensory organs of the tongue and palate, distinguishing salty, sweet, sour, and bitter tastes.

Teeth Bonelike structures in the jaws. Different types (incisors, canines, premolars, molars) are specialized to tear, crush, and/or grind food.
Tendons Bands of fibrous connective tissue joining muscles to bones.
Testis (*or* Testicle) One of a pair of primary male sex organs that manufacture sperm (plural: testes).
Thalamus A brain structure above the hypothalamus. It sends sensory impulses to the cerebral cortex, links sensations with emotions, and affects consciousness.
Thymus An endocrine gland located behind the sternum. It produces thymosin.
Thyroid An endocrine gland at the front of the neck, producing thyroid hormone.
Tissue A collection of similar cells that perform a particular task.
Trachea (*or* Windpipe) The tube between the larynx and the bronchi.
Tubule A tiny tube.
Tunica A tissue layer forming a coating. Blood vessels have three such layers (intima, media, adventitia).
Unstriated muscle *See* **Smooth muscle**.
Ureter The tube conveying urine from a kidney to the bladder.
Urethra The passage taking urine from the bladder to the body's exterior.
Urinary system The kidneys, ureters, bladder, and urethra.
Urine Liquid waste excreted by the kidneys.
Uterine tubes *See* **Fallopian tubes**.
Uterus (*or* Womb) A hollow muscular organ located above the bladder. Inside it, a fertilized ovum develops into a fetus.
Uvula A conical tag hanging from the back of the palate. It helps to keep food out of the nasal cavities.
Vagina The muscular passage between the vulva and cervix (neck of the uterus).
Vascular Relating to or richly supplied with vessels, especially blood vessels.
Vein A blood vessel that transports blood from capillaries back to the heart. Veins contain valves to prevent the backflow of blood.
Venous Relating to veins.
Ventricle A cavity: one of the two lower chambers of the heart.
Venule A small vein.
Vermiform appendix *See* **Appendix**.
Vertebra A bone of the vertebral column (plural: vertebrae).
Vertebral column (*or* Backbone *or* Spine) The column of vertebrae between the skull and the hip bones, supporting the body and shielding the spinal cord. It has five sections: cervical, thoracic, lumbar, sacral, and coccygeal.
Vestibule A space before a passage begins, as in the inner ear beyond the oval window, between the semicircular ducts and cochlea.
Vocal cords Two belts of tissue stretched across the larynx which produce sounds when air rushes past them.
Vulva (*or* Pudendum) The external female genitals.
White matter The paler tissue of the brain and spinal cord comprised mainly of myelin-sheathed nerve fibers.
Windpipe *See* **Trachea**.
Womb *See* **Uterus**.

© DIAGRAM

Web sites to visit

There is a lot of useful information on the internet. There are also many sites that are fun to use. Remember that you may be able to get information on a particular topic by using a search engine such as Google (**http://www.google.com**). Some of the sites that are found in this way may be very useful, others not. Below is a selection of Web sites related to the material covered by this book. Most are illustrated, and they are mainly of the type that provides useful facts.

Facts On File, Inc. *takes no responsibility for the information contained within these Web sites. All the sites were accessible in January 2005.*

Anatomy of the Human Body : Gray's Anatomy
Online version of the classic *Gray's Anatomy of the Human Body*, containing over 13,000 entries and 1,200 images.
http://www.bartleby.com/107/

Biology Online
A source for biological information, suitable for homework, research projects, and general interest, with hundreds of biology Web site links.
http://www.biology-online.org/

BIOME
A guide to selected, quality-checked internet resources in the health and life sciences.
http://biome.ac.uk/

Health Sciences and Human Services Library
Provides links to selected Web sites that may be useful to both students and researchers.
http://www.hshsl.umaryland.edu/resources/lifesciences.html

Human Anatomy Online
Interactive resource, with visual keys to text on the human body.
http://www.innerbody.com

North Harris College Biology Department
Tutorials and graphics on biology, human anatomy, human physiology, microbiology, and nutrition.
http://science.nhmccd.edu/biol/

Open Directory Project: Reproductive Health
Comprehensive list of internet resources.
http://dmoz.org/Health/Reproductive_Health/

Open Directory Project: Teen life: Sexuality
Comprehensive list of internet resources.
http://dmoz.org/Kids_and_Teens/Teen_Life/Sexuality/

The Biology Project
Structured tutorials on life sciences. Particularly strong on cell biology, human biology, and molecular biology.
http://www.biology.arizona.edu

University of Texas: BioTech Life Sciences Resources and Reference Tools
Enriching knowledge of biology and chemistry, for everyone from high school students to professional researchers. The Dictionary and Science Resources are particularly useful.
http://biotech.icmb.utexas.edu

A
abortion 39, 88
acne 20
Adam's apple 19
adolescence 18, 19, 20, 21
amnion 14, 66, 68
  twins 78, 79
amniotic fluid 14
  labor 93
  placenta 74
  pregnancy 61
  testing 67
androgens 16

B
birth 22, 23, 92–97
  menstruation 39
  positions 96
  problems 97
blastocyst 14, 15, 23, 65, 66, 68
  placenta 74
  pregnancy 58
  twins 79
blood supply 7, 25, 47
body odor 20
Braxton-Hick contractions 77
breastfeeding 40
breasts (mammary glands) 6, 7, 10, 11, 34–35
  hormones 17
  pregnancy 59, 81
  puberty 18, 38
breech birth 14, 95, 97

C
cancer
  breast 35
  female reproductive problems 37, 39
  male reproductive problems 54, 55, 56
  sexual problems 89
cervix 6, 10, 14, 23, 24
  female reproductive problems 37, 42, 43
  labor 93, 94
  pregnancy 76, 77
  sexual problems 88
cesarean birth 97
child development 100–101
chorion 14, 66, 68
  twins 78, 79
chromosomes 15
  oogenesis 26, 27
  sex determination 92
  sperm production 48, 49
  zygote development 64
circulation, baby 75, 95
circumcision 13, 55, 89
clitoris 6, 8, 10, 22, 23, 24
  sexual problems 88
condom 86, 87, 90, 91
contraception 86–87
contraceptive device 39, 41, 86–87, 88
contraceptive pill 41, 86
corpus luteum 10, 11, 17, 28, 29, 32
Cowper's gland 12, 13, 52, 57
cystitis 37

D
dartos muscle 12, 50
delivery 94–95, 97
displaced uterus 37
dysmenorrhea 41

E
ejaculation 6
  contraception 87
  female reproductive problems 42
  male reproductive system 9, 12, 13, 44, 45, 46
  puberty 18, 19
  sexual problems 89
  sperm production 48
embryo 6, 8, 14, 15, 30
  development 65, 66, 68–69
  miscarriage 83
  pregnancy 58, 60
  twins 78, 79
endocrine glands 10, 16, 29
endometrium 30, 31
  embryo development 66, 68
  female reproductive system 10, 42, 43
  fertilization 63
  labor 95
  menstrual cycle 32, 33
  pregnancy 58
epididymis 6, 9, 12, 13, 45, 46, 50, 51
  male reproductive problems 56
  sperm production 48, 49
erectile tissue
  female 6, 10, 24
  male 12, 13, 44, 52, 53
  sexual problems 89
erection 13, 44, 53
  puberty 54
  sexual problems 57, 89, 91
estrogen 8, 10, 17, 23
  female reproductive problems 42

menstrual cycle 32, 33
ovaries 28, 29
excretory system 24, 46
exercise
menstruation 40, 41
pregnancy 83, 84–85

F
fallopian tubes (oviducts) 6, 8, 10, 23, 24, 30, 31
blood supply 25
female reproductive problems 37, 39, 42
fertilization 62, 63
sexual problems 88
zygote development 65
female reproductive system 6, 8, 22–43
problems 42–43
fertilization (conception) 6, 14, 62–63
accessory organs 30
female reproductive system 8, 22, 23, 42
male reproductive system 9
oogenesis 26, 27
pregnancy 58
twins 78, 79
zygote development 64
fetus 6, 7, 14
circulation 75
development 69–73
female reproductive system 8, 22, 23
full term 76–77
labor 93
miscarriage 83
placenta 74
position for birth 95, 96
pregnancy 58, 59, 60
fibroids 42
follicle-stimulating hormone (FSH) 10, 11, 28, 29, 32
foreskin (prepuce) 12, 53
problems 54, 55, 89

G
gametes (sex cells) 8, 49
female 10, 14
male 9, 12, 48
genetic material 7, 27, 48, 62, 78, 79
genitals
female 6, 8, 24, 36
fetus development 70
male 6, 12, 44, 45, 46, 47
problems 20, 91
puberty 18, 19
germ cells 14, 48
glans 12, 44, 52, 53, 55, 89
gonadotrophins 10
gonads
female 8, 10, 24
male 12, 16, 44
growth
child development 101
male hormones 16
newborn babies 99
puberty 18, 19

H
hair
female hormones 17
male hormones 16
puberty 18, 19, 38, 54
heavy periods 39, 40, 41
hernia 55, 56
hormones 16–17
contraception 86
female 8, 10, 11, 23, 42, 80
fetus development 70
labor 95
male 9, 13, 45, 54, 56
menstrual cycle 32, 38, 39, 40, 41
ovaries 28, 29
pregnancy 59
puberty 18, 20
sexual problems 42, 89, 91
hygiene 36, 54
hymen 11, 22, 88
hypothalamus 16, 17, 32, 39, 41
hysterectomy 37

I
implantation 15
accessory organs 30
contraception 86
embryo development 66
female reproductive system 17, 42
menstrual cycle 32, 33
pregnancy 58
impotence 57, 91
infection
breast 34
contraception 87
female reproductive problems 36, 37, 42
male reproductive problems 54, 56
sexual problems 88, 90–91
infertility 42, 56, 88, 89
infestations 43, 57, 90
intrauterine device (IUD) 39, 41, 86–87, 88

L
labia 6, 8, 10, 11, 22, 23, 24, 88

labor 14, 15, 92, 93–95
accessory organs 31
female hormones 17
full term fetus 76, 77
mother's age 80
pregnancy 61
lactation 11
larynx 16, 19
luteinizing hormone (LH) 11, 32

M

male reproductive system 6, 9, 44–57
blood supply 47
problems 54–57
meiosis 15, 26, 27, 48
menopause 11, 35, 41, 80, 91
menstruation (periods) 10, 11, 23, 31, 86
cycle 17, 22, 32–33
pregnancy 59, 60, 80, 81
problems 20, 37, 38–39, 40–41, 42
puberty 18
milk 6, 7, 11, 17, 34–35
miscarriage 37, 83
mitosis 15, 26, 48, 63, 64
morning sickness 59, 60, 67, 81, 83, 64
morula 15, 65
mucus 22, 23, 43, 77, 94

N

newborn baby 95, 98–99
nipple 6, 10, 11, 34, 35
puberty 18, 38

O

oocyte 26, 29
oogenesis 26, 27
orgasm 12, 13, 22, 54
sexual problems 91
ovarian (Graafian) follicle 10–11, 28, 29
fertilization 63
hormones 17
menstrual cycle 32
ovaries 6, 7, 8, 10, 11, 17, 22, 23, 24, 30
blood supply 25
fertilization 63
oogenesis 26
problems 38, 39, 42, 43, 88, 91
puberty 18, 38
structure 28
ovulation 8, 11, 17, 30, 38
contraception 86
fertilization 63
menstrual cycle 32
ovarian cycle 29
ovum (egg) 6, 7, 8, 9, 10, 11, 22, 23, 30
chromosomes 49
development 64–65
fertilization 62, 63
menstrual cycle 32, 33, 38
oogenesis 26, 27
ovaries 28, 29
pregnancy 58, 60
problems 38, 42
sex determination 92
twins 78, 79

P

penis 6, 7, 9, 12, 13, 44, 45, 46, 52–53
contraception 87
problems 54, 55, 57, 89, 90
puberty 19
perineum 11, 12, 24
pituitary gland 10, 11, 16, 17, 28, 29, 32, 39
sexual problems 89
placenta 6, 7, 8, 11, 14, 15, 67, 74–75
development 65, 68, 76
fertilization 63
labor 95
menstrual cycle 32
twins 78, 79
pregnancy (gestation) 8, 15, 67, 58–85
breast 35
diet 82, 83
exercise 84–85
female hormones 17
fetus development 69–73
mother's age 80
problems 37, 40, 41, 42, 61, 80–83
signs 59, 64
trimesters 60–61
premature babies 61
premenstrual tension 38–39, 40
prenatal care 82
progesterone 8, 11, 17, 23, 28, 32
problems 39, 42
prostate gland 6, 12, 13, 45, 46
problems 54, 56, 57, 89, 91
puberty 19, 54
puberty 18–19, 21, 80
breast 35
female hormones 17
oogenesis 26
problems 20–21, 38, 54
sperm production 48

S

scrotum 6, 9, 12, 13, 44, 45, 46, 50
  blood supply 47
  hormones 16
  problems 54, 55, 56, 91
secondary sexual characteristics 10
semen 6, 9, 12, 13, 44, 45, 46
  contraception 87
  female reproductive system 22, 42
  problems 42, 54, 57
  sperm production 48
  volume 51
seminal fluid 6, 12, 13
  problems 91
seminal vesicles 6, 9, 12, 13, 45
  problems 56, 57, 89
seminiferous tubules 48, 49, 51, 91
sex determination 92
sexual intercourse (copulation) 12, 22, 23, 45
  pregnancy 67
  problems 36, 37, 54, 57, 88–89, 91
sexually transmitted (venereal) diseases (STDs) 43, 56, 90
sperm (spermatozoa) 6, 7, 9, 12, 13, 15, 44, 45, 46, 51
  contraception 87
  female reproductive system 23, 30, 42
  fertilization 62, 63, 92
  gametes 49
  hormones 16
  penis 52
  pregnancy 58
  problems 42, 54, 55, 56, 57
  production (spermatogenesis) 27, 48–49
  puberty 54
  twins 78, 79
  zygote development 64
stroma 28

T

testes 6, 7, 9, 12, 13, 44, 45, 46, 50–51
  blood supply 47
  hormones 16
  problems 54, 55, 56, 89, 91
  puberty 54
  sperm production 48, 49
testosterone 9, 12, 13, 16, 45
  problems 54
tumors 34, 35, 39, 42, 43, 56
twins 78–79, 80

U

umbilical cord 15, 74, 75
  embryo 66, 68
  labor 94, 95
  twins 78
urethritis 57
uterus (womb) 6, 7, 8, 10, 11, 22, 23, 24
  accessory organs 30, 31
  birth 15, 92, 93, 94
  blood supply 25
  fertilization 63
  hormones 17
  menstrual cycle 32, 33
  pregnancy 58, 59, 60, 65, 69, 70, 76, 83
  problems 37, 39, 42, 43, 83, 88, 91
  puberty 38

V

vagina (birth canal) 6, 7, 8, 10, 11, 22, 23, 24
  accessory organs 31
  birth 15, 92, 94
  hormones 17
  menstrual cycle 33
  pregnancy 61
  problems 37, 38, 42, 43, 88, 91
  puberty 18
vas deferens 6, 9, 13, 45, 46, 50, 56
  sterilization 87
vertex presentation 15, 96
vestibular glands 6, 22, 23
vulva (pudendum) 6, 8, 11, 22, 23, 24
  problems 36, 37, 43, 88, 90, 91
  puberty 18

Z

zona pellucida 15
zygote 8, 14, 15, 22, 23
  development 64, 65
  fertilization 62, 63